THE PENGUIN POETS

POEM INTO POEM

WORLD POETRY IN MODERN VERSE

TRANSLATION

POEM INTO POEM

WORLD POETRY IN MODERN VERSE
TRANSLATION

INTRODUCED AND EDITED BY
George Steiner

PENGUIN BOOKS

Penguin Books Ltd, Harmondsworth, Middlesex, England
Penguin Books Inc., 7110 Ambassador Road, Baltimore, Maryland 21207, U.S.A.
Penguin Books Australia Ltd, Ringwood, Victoria, Australia

—

First published under the title
The Penguin Book of Modern Verse Translation 1966
Reissued as *Poem into Poem* 1970

—

Copyright © George Steiner, 1966, 1970

—

Made and printed in Great Britain by
Cox & Wyman Ltd
London, Reading and Fakenham
Set in Monotype Fournier

CONTENTS

CONTENTS

CONTENTS

CONTENTS

CONTENTS

CONTENTS

CONTENTS

CONTENTS

CONTENTS

CONTENTS

CONTENTS

INTRODUCTION

THAT it is untranslatable is one of the definitions offered of poetry. What remains after the attempt, intact and uncommunicated, is the original poem. So affirmed du Bellay, the French poet and rhetorician of the early sixteenth century, so, more recently, Robert Frost. A poem is language in the most intense mode of expressive integrity, language under such close pressure of singular need, of particularized energy, that no other statement can be equivalent, that no other poem even if it differs only in one phrase, perhaps one word, can do the same job. The poem is because nothing exactly like it has been before, because its very composition is an act of unique designation, of naming some previously anonymous or inchoate experience as Adam named the creatures of life. A painting divides space between self and the whole; so a poem divides experience between itself and 'otherness'. How can identity be translated into anything but itself? This is the admonition of Borges's acid fable of a man translating *Don Quixote* into identical Spanish, line by line and word for word.

Add to this the nature of poetic language. The distinctive beat of any given tongue, that sustaining undercurrent of inflexion, pitch relations, habits of stress, which give a particular motion to prose, is concentrated in poetry so that it acts as an overt, characteristic force. Poetry will not translate any more than music. Verse forms, the shape of the stanza, the conventional or innovating directives of rhyme, the historical, stylistic discriminations which a language makes between its prosaic and poetic idiom, the counterpoint it sets up between colloquial and formal, these also defy translation. As does the immediate visual code of long and short words, of capitalization and accentual mark in German, say, or Spanish. And how can a translation carry over into a Roman alphabet the pictorial suggestions, the relations of space and graphic incitement which are a vital part of the total statement made by a Chinese or Persian lyric?

In short: because a poem enlists the maximal range of linguistic means, because it articulates the code of any given language at its most incisive – all other poems in that language being a part of the informing context – poetry may be paraphrased, imperfectly mimed but 'indeed cannot be translated'. To which Dr Johnson adds, 'and therefore it is the poet that preserves language'.

But let us observe the argument closely. It cuts much deeper than verse. It implicates even rudimentary acts of linguistic exchange, the attempt to translate any word or sentence from one language into another. A language is not a passive representation of reality, it does not restrict itself to being a mirror. It is an active world image, selecting certain possibilities of human analysis and behaviour, certain ways of initiating, structuring and recording experience from a total potentiality of representation. Each language cuts out its segment of reality. We live our world as we speak it (to ourselves or to others), as it feeds back to us through the particular linguistic code most immediate to our culture and personal up-bringing. We cast the net of our own language over the multiplicity of living forms. Loosely woven, it will draw in experience in gross, indiscriminate lumps; the landscape of being is made incoherent and monotonous by illiterate speech. Close knit, the language-net makes available to us the largest possible range – possible to our physiological and historical condition – of differentiated, mastered, potentially related elements.

A large vocabulary signifies a literal wealth and concreteness of felt life. A developed syntax engenders those perceptions of interrelation, those creative re-groupings of thought and action called metaphor. Without metaphor a society remains static, repetitive, as is a child's song. Our world, the way we move among its total possibilities, springs from grammar, from the pattern by which we relate identity, verb and object. Each grammar differs in some degree from any other. Thus there is not the same life-image in *j'ai mal à la tête* as in *mi duole il capo*. Neither is exactly equivalent, though one is nearer than the other, to *I have a headache*. No two languages mesh perfectly, no two languages – and there may be some three thousand spoken by men – set the world in the same order.

Even the simplest words, indeed they especially, carry a charge of specific energy, of historical association, social usage and syntactic tradition. They rise to the surface of speech from great depths of national or regional sensibility, barnacled with undeclared remembrance. *Pain* is not wholly rendered by *bread*. It has to a French ear resonances of want, of radical demand, which the English word does not; the two words differ in historical texture as does a French from an English loaf. There is no synonym in either French or English for German *heimat* (though *terroir* carries some of the relevant overtones). The interweaving of concrete and spiritual patrimony, of obligation and pride, concentrated in the German term has no full equivalent in the English vocabulary nor, through crucial, necessary correspondence of idiom with world-image, in English historical and political practice. We can define the Greek optative as a mode of the verb articulating wish, desire, uncertain hope; but no optative can be completely reproduced in a grammar, one would almost say in a metaphysic, which lacks this particular shade of futurity. Or to cite an example familiar to Biblical translation: as there is no concept of snow, hence no word for it, in a number of African languages, the conventional equivalent for *white as snow* is *white as egret feathers*. This 'equivalent' is entirely devoid of the tactile, emotive overtones, of the latent metaphors of chill, shrouding action, even of the colour-spectrum associated with our Middle-English, ultimately Sanskrit word.

There are no total translations: because languages differ, because each language represents a complex, historically and collectively determined aggregate of values, proceedings of social conduct, conjectures on life. There can be no exhaustive transfer from language A to language B, no meshing of nets so precise that there is identity of conceptual content, unison of undertone, absolute symmetry of aural and visual association. This is true both of a simple prose statement and of poetry.

The point is worth stressing. Where they engage, as they must, the root fact of linguistic autonomy, the fact that different grammars delineate different realities, arguments against verse translation are arguments against all translation. The difference is one of intensity, of technical difficulty, of psychological apprehension. Because a poem springs from the core of a language, commemorating and renewing the world view of that language at its deepest level, the risks taken in translation are greater, the waste or damage done more visible. But a gritty colloquialism will frequently offer a resistance as vital and obstinate.

Each act of translation is one of approximation, of near miss or failure to get within range. It tells of our fragmented legacy, and of the marvellous richness of that legacy – how meagre must the earth have been before Babel, when all spoke alike and communicated on the instant. The case against translation is irrefutable, but only if we are presented, in Ibsen's phrase, with 'the claims of the ideal'.

In actual performance these claims cannot be met or allowed.

They have been discarded, obviously, in our economic, political, private affairs. Men's undertakings proceed by linguistic barter in a zone of approximate, utilitarian definition. School primers, tourists' phrase-books, manuals of commercial and technical usage, our ordinary lexica, establish a neutral ground of rough-edged but indispensable concordance. The multiplicity of scientific developments, the fact that science operates internationally and at its own forward edge, have made of the translation of scientific papers a large-scale, urgent enterprise. Some of the difficulties met resemble those which arise in the translation of poetry, the main difference being that mathematics is a true esperanto, a perfectly conventional yet dynamic code such as no artificial or inter-language can be.

Translation is equally essential to humanism, to the continued life of feeling. We translate perpetually – this is often overlooked – when we read a classic in our own tongue, a poem written in the sixteenth century or a novel published in 1780. We seek to recapture, to revitalize in our consciousness the meanings of words used as we no longer use them, of imaginings that have behind them a contour of history, of manners, of religious or philosophic presumptions radically different from ours. Anyone reading Donne or Jane Austen today, or almost any poem or fiction composed before 1915 (at about which date the old order seems to recede from the immediate grasp of our sensibility), is trying to re-create by exercise of historical, linguistic response; he is, in the full sense, translating. As is the player who acts Shakespeare or Congreve, making that which was conceived in a society, in a style of feeling, in an expressive convention sharply different from that of the modern, actual, active to the touch of our mind and nerve.

No language, moreover, however comprehensive, however resourceful and inclusive its syntax, covers more than a fraction of human realization. There are, at every moment and on every horizon worlds beyond our own words. Hence the urge to cross the barriers of national speech, the effort to make other insights, other tools of awareness, available. What man has the linguistic wealth needed to read in the original Homer, the Bible, Shakespeare, Pascal, *The Brothers Karamazov*, the poems of Li Po and *A Tale of the Genji*? Yet which would one be prepared to do without or discard from the adventure of literacy? A major, perhaps a predominant element in our culture, in the fabric of our consciousness, is inevitably translation. 'Say what one will of its inadequacy,' wrote Goethe to Carlyle, 'translation remains one of the most important, worthwhile concerns in the totality of world affairs.' Without it we would live in arrogant parishes bordered by silence.

So much will probably be allowed by almost anyone. But what of the more special argument that poetry should not be translated into poetry – that the only honest translation of a poem is a literal trot or a prose paraphrase? This is clearly implied in Dante's statement, 'nothing which is harmonized by the bond of the Muses can be changed from its own to another language without having all its sweetness destroyed'. It is the conclusion arrived at by Sir Richard Burton when considering the translation of Arabic verse. Today it is put most drastically by Nabokov: 'The clumsiest literal translation is a thousand times more useful than the prettiest paraphrase.' To say that Dante and Nabokov have themselves produced brilliant verse translation, that the art of poetic translation is almost as old as poetry itself, that it continues intensely alive, is true enough. But it is no refutation. The case for the interlinear or the prose paraphrase is, in fact, a strong one.

It can be met only if the exercise of poetic translation exhibits advantages, means of critical understanding, qualities of linguistic gain which no prose version matches. It must be shown that there is even in the inevitable compromise of verse translation, even in its necessary defeats – perhaps characteristically in these – a creative residue, a margin of experienced if not fully communicated illumination which no trot or prose statement offers. It is precisely this, I think, which *can* be shown. A 'clumsy literal translation' of a living poem is none at all; a prose paraphrase is an important auxiliary, but no more. To find active echo, a poem must incite to a poem.

Because it is unalterably itself in its own language, a poem yields little of its genius to prose. Though there are styles (the neo-classic for instance) which appropriate the sinew and directness of prose, the two media are in essence different. The poem does not accept the routine and short-hand of experience set down in prose, thinned out in the mainly inert figures of daily speech; by constant definition the poem works against the grain of the ordinary. This creative insurgence is the very start of the poem; the poet seeks to scandalize our acceptances, to make new and rebellious. Thus even at its most spacious a prose paraphrase signifies a good deal less to a poem than does a piano transcription to an orchestral score.

Consider this passage from Book VI of the *Iliad* (Glaukos' answer to Diomedes' war-challenge):

> Like leaves on trees the race of man is found,
> Now green in youth, now withering on the ground;
> Another race the following spring supplies;
> They fall successive, and successive rise:
> So generations in their course decay;
> So flourish these, when those are passed away.
> But if thou still persist to search my birth,
> Then hear a tale that fills the spacious earth.

> As is the generation of leaves, so is that of humanity.
> The wind scatters the leaves on the ground, but the live timber
> burgeons with leaves again in the season of spring returning.
> So one generation of men will grow while another
> dies. Yet if you wish to learn all this and be certain
> of my genealogy: there are plenty of men who know it.

Men in their generation are like the leaves of the trees. The wind blows and one year's leaves are scattered on the ground; but the trees burst into bud and put on fresh ones when the spring comes round. In the same way one generation flourishes and another nears its end. But if you wish to hear about my family, I will tell you the tale – most people know it already.

Pope's is undoubtedly the most satisfactory of the three versions, for its discipline and alert pace; the fourth line illustrates how the energy of precise etymology – Pope's confident control of the Latinate *successive* – quickens our entire imaginative response, so that we very nearly experience a graphic action. But it is the best version primarily because Pope's idiom is most fully committed to the fact that the *Iliad* is a poem, that its design and effect are poetic. For all its formulaic scruple, Richmond Lattimore's text is, at this particular point, far less persuasive; and this so exactly in the measure in which its looser syntax and vocabulary incline to the very different precisions or contractions of prose (*genealogy: there are plenty of men who know it*). E. V. Rieu's translation is by much the feeblest of the three. Inspired by the wish – at the time almost a social, expressly didactic motive – to make Homer widely popular, to present the *Iliad* as a timeless yarn, Rieu sacrificed poetic form to an agile, colloquial prose. But not altogether; Rieu's uneasiness about the enterprise leads, in the passage quoted, to the bits of interior rhyme (*ground*/*round*, *year's*/*nears*) and 'fossil' cadences of blank verse, both damaging.

The point is simply this: though always imperfect, a verse translation, in that it re-presents, re-enacts that selection of language, that stylization or innovation of syntax inseparable from the nature of poetic composition, is more responsible to the intent, to the movement of spirit in the original than a downward transfer into prose can ever be.

This example makes a second point. Each time a poem is translated, initiating a new poem, the original finds new and active life in present awareness. Translation gives to the metaphor of classic survival, of the unbroken forward-acting role of literature a solid reality. As it could in no other way, the Homeric epic, in the uninterrupted sequence of translations from Chapman and Hobbes to Robert Fitzgerald and Christopher Logue, is at work in English literature, is interwoven with the fabric of the language and of the English and American poetic tradition. Verse re-presentations of Horace and Catullus are fully implicit in the development of English satire, of the English domestic lyric and love poem. Shakespearean translation is crucially a part of the late growth, of the coming to self-confidence, of German classic and romantic verse. The classic wanes to the status of the academic or falls silent unless it is re-appropriated by translation, unless the living poet examines and affirms its relevance to the current idiom (for want of vital translation Lucretius is, at present, inert).

But poetic translation is not only a living spark, a flow of energy between past and present and between cultures (immersion, so far as we may experience it, in another language being as close as we can come to a second self, to breaking free of the habitual skin or tortoise-shell of our consciousness); poetic translation plays a unique role inside the translator's own speech. It drives inward. Anyone translating a poem, or attempting to, is brought face to face, as by no other exercise, with the genius, bone-structure and limitations of his native tongue. Because that tongue is our constant landscape, we almost grow oblivious to its horizon, we take it to be the only or privileged space of being. Translation taxes and thus makes inventory of our resources. It compels us to realize that there are raw materials

we lack, stocks of feeling, instruments of expression, inlets to aware-
ness which our own linguistic territory does not possess or has failed
to exploit. This last recognition can be a powerful stimulus: witness
Baudelaire's and Mallarmé's determination to import from Poe a
brand of unreason and murky brilliance which they felt lacking in
French, or Goethe's efforts to bend a European language towards the
greater multiplicity of erotic nuance, of amorous-philosophic con-
gruence which he had observed in oriental poetry. Poetic translation
enriches by what it reveals of our poverties.

Its necessary failures, the fact that the original cannot be
rendered exhaustively, that we cannot retrace the steps of the poet
had he conceived the poem in our own language, are often uniquely
positive. The inadequacies of a significant translation are creative of
insight, critically revealing as no other reading of a poem is. To the
poet who translates and to the reader who has access to both lan-
guages that is the justifying paradox. What remains uncommunicated
after translation is not *the poem* or even its essential elements. Depend-
ing on the case, what fails to come across may be structures of spirit
peculiar to the original language, networks of historical or phonetic
association, a grid of immediate symbolic recognitions or idiomatic
shorthand unrecapturable because they are so firmly localized in a
specific cultural milieu, society, historical epoch remote from our
own. No translation by a later poet (unless, perhaps, he is working
from an African or aboriginal context) can simulate the collective,
orally conceived resonance of Homeric formulae. Dante's difficulties
and good fortune in composing, literally, a new vulgate, cannot be
fully mirrored in any translation using a language already established
and burdened with poetic precedent. The relative interchangeability
of the parts of speech in a German sentence, of which Rilke makes a
means of suspended motion and contrary definition, will not pass into
French syntax.

But each of these defeats is creative. It penetrates and identifies the
genius of the original; it communicates that genius to us by what it
fails to re-produce. A great poetic translation – Hölderlin's Sopho-
kles, Valéry's restatement of Virgil's *Eclogues*, Robert Lowell's
readings of Heine – is criticism in the highest sense. It surrounds
the original with a zone of unmastered meaning, an area in which
the original declares its own singular life. It is the job of all genuine
literary criticism to fall short, to make explicit by its own precisely

honest inadequacy, the genius of that it focuses on. The piece of criticism accumulates whatever linguistic, historical, referential insights it can command and make relevant; but it must show in the process that this accumulation comes to less than the sum of the poem. What the poem says criticism cannot fully restate; criticism is most valid where it makes the margin of difference lucid, where it draws around the work of the poet a barrier of light.

The poetic translator does the same, but goes deeper because he takes larger risks. The circle he traces around the original illumines not only the text he is translating but his own art and person. In Roy Campbell's versions of Baudelaire we note a three-fold action and radical honesty: a re-presentment of Baudelaire's poems, a critical perception of the genius of those poems by virtue of what is incomplete in the translation, and a necessary disclosure of what may be facile or coarse-grained in Campbell's own idiom. The process of perceptive engagement is strictly comparable only to that which occurs when a composer sets a major poem, when Britten, for example, 'translates' Blake or Rimbaud.

At its best, the peculiar synthesis of conflict and complicity between a poem and its translation into another poem creates the impression of a 'third language', of a medium of communicative energy which somehow reconciles both languages in a tongue deeper, more comprehensive than either. In the no-man's-land between du Bellay's *Heureux qui comme Ulysse* and Chesterton's English sonnet, so nearly exhaustive of the original, we seem to hear *'encore l'immortelle parole'*, Mallarmé's expression for the notion of a universal, immediate tongue from which English and French had broken off. This experience of what the German critic Walter Benjamin termed a 'lost totality', an underlying unison in the mystery of human speech, is the ideal towards which translation strives. It cannot be fulfilled. Translations range from those which traduce to those which transfigure. Transfiguration, the version which surpasses the original as Baudelaire excels Poe, is perhaps the more lasting betrayal. But the attempt to translate must be made, the risks taken, if that tower in Babel is to be more than ruin. It has been made, with particular wealth and vigour, in the period from *c.* 1870 to the present.

2

What follows is a selection of translations by English and American poets of poetry from twenty-two languages. It begins with Gladstone's rendition of Horace III, 30, published in 1863, as fair illustration of the old style, and extends to 1965 with a previously unpublished translation of Neruda.

The first principle of selection has been that the English or American poem should have a distinct autonomy, that it should be worth reading in its own right. A good number of these verse translations rank with the best poetry written in English in our time. Secondarily, this anthology seeks to indicate the history of modern poetic translation, the passage from Victorian 'classic paraphrase' to what Robert Lowell, as did Dryden and Ben Jonson before him, calls 'imitation'. It also tries to suggest how classic, Oriental, French or Spanish poetry have interacted with the development of the modern Anglo-American verse idiom. But the historical consideration which would, for instance, have called for the inclusion of Witter Bynner's *Iphigenia in Tauris* (1915), a decisive document in the growth of the modern tone, has been secondary to that of pleasure, of the wish to show what fine poetry has come of the dialogue between languages, cultures and historical periods.

A few texts have been omitted because permission to republish has not been given: among them Nabokov's exquisite translations of lyrics by Pushkin, Lermontov and Tyutchev. Legal convention allows me to smuggle in one stanza:

> Soft sand comes up to our horses' shanks
>   as we ride in the darkening day
> and the shadows of pines have closed their ranks:
>   all is shadow along our way.

I am conscious of the omission of translations from African and American Indian song and poetry, a field in which Sir Maurice Bowra has been a pioneer, and which is beginning to modify our notion of world literature. I have also left out translations from the Persian and Arabic; perhaps wrongly, I feel that those I have seen move in a saccharine limbo between the original and the natural shapes of English. With one brief exception, I have found myself discarding translations of Pindar, Hölderlin and Leopardi. These three poets seem to mark the limits of possible re-statement. Translations do not throw light on them but a penumbra.

The main ground for omission, however, has been quite simply and brutally lack of space. It would not be difficult to fill a volume twice this size. With several interesting exceptions such as Dylan Thomas, who knew no other language, and Wallace Stevens, whose uses of English were deliberately permeable to the insinuations of Latin, French and Italian, there is scarcely an important English or American poet since the Victorians who has not been a translator as well. Periodicals such as *Nine* and *Arion* have been devoted largely to poetic translation and to the theory and problems of the art. As I write, a new journal concerned exclusively with the translation of foreign verse into English is being started in London. The period from Rossetti to Robert Lowell has been an age of poetic translation rivalling that of the Tudor and Elizabethan masters. In range of linguistic response it has clearly surpassed the sixteenth century. Why should this be?

There is no single, obvious answer. A contrary force has been at work in the modern sensibility: a hunger for lineage, for informing tradition, and a simultaneous impulse to make all things new. Both currents would lead to the revaluation and 'modernization' of classic and medieval literature. There has also been a characteristic internationalization of the poetic temper. We find in the work of Eliot, Pound, Apollinaire, Valéry, Rilke, Mayakovsky, Neruda, a shared logic of emotion, an agreed code of reference and symbolic device. Modern poets are alert to each other's performance; much modern verse is directly or by force of echo filled with cross-reference to other poetry, to other cultures. Poetic translation is the most open, deliberate mode of reference.

The instability of contemporary norms, the tendency to regard our morals and canons of taste as purely relative or provisional, has meant that alien cultures, alien conventions of feeling, exercise a peculiar fascination on the western mind. The Javanese tone sequence in a Debussy score, the African mask in a Picasso, the translations of Hindi or Nigerian lyrics into English verse, embody a common appetite for renewal, for the vitalizing shock, and a common guilt towards that which we have too long pillaged or scorned as mere colonizers.

There appear to be economic and sociological factors in the brilliance and profusion of modern poetic translation, particularly in America (Marianne Moore, Richmond Lattimore, Robert Lowell, Richard Wilbur, Robert Fitzgerald, William Arrowsmith). In American culture the desire for tradition, for precedent, in the classic past, collides with a widespread ignorance of foreign languages and history. Few know Greek in Athens (Georgia) or Latin in Rome (Illinois). Yet the sentiment that Homer and Juvenal are part of the status of civilized consciousness remains genuine. It has found an influential economic and technological ally in the activities of the American university campus and in the hunger of the paperback. To keep the machines fed, paperback publishers have raided the past and the foreign (half a dozen versions of Homer in the last ten years). Like the BBC in England, American academic and commercial editors have directly commissioned much of the best of recent verse translation. Robert Fitzgerald's *Odyssey*, William Merwin's Spanish ballads, the versions of Greek drama by Arrowsmith and the Chicago group, were made possible by this new patronage and the mass-market of the campus bookstore.

As important as all these reasons put together, however, and central to the manner and controversial liberties of the modern form, is the achievement of one man. If our age of poetic translation rivals that of Golding, Gavin Douglas and Chapman, it is because of the teaching and example of Ezra Pound.

The whole of Pound's writing may be seen as an act of translation, as the appropriation to an idiom radically his own of a fantastic ragbag of languages, cultural legacies, historical echoes, stylistic models. 'To consider Pound's original work and his translation separately,' notes Eliot, 'would be a mistake, a mistake which implies a greater mistake about the nature of translation.' Pound has been the master jackdaw in the museum and scrap-heap of civilization, the courier between far places of the mind, the contriver of a chaotic patchwork of values which, on decisive occasion, and by some great gift of irascible love, fuse into a strange coherence. As A. Alvarez has said, Pound manages to write English verse as if Shakespeare had not written before him, a scandal and liberation made possible by his raids on Provençal and French, on Latin and Chinese (be it off the silk-scroll or the tea-crate), on Whitman and Heine. Within this general plunder, Pound's actual translations play a vital part. They have altered the definition and ideals of verse translation in the twentieth century as surely as Pound's poetry has renewed or subverted modern English and American poetics.

A first look at nearly any translation in this anthology is enough to show whether it comes before or after the *Homage to Sextus Propertius* (1917/1934). But the 'making new' of translation had already occurred in *Personae* (1909) and *Provença* (1910). After 'The River Merchant's Wife' (1915) the art of translation had entered its modern phase.

Pound's actual repertoire and range of enthusiasm were not as novel as might appear. The focus on the Greek lyrics, on Catullus, on Provençal and Tuscan poetry, on Villon, Baudelaire and Verlaine had already been defined by the Victorian translators, by Rossetti, Swinburne, Arthur Symons and Ernest Dowson. Arthur Waley, four years younger than Pound, was at work independently, shaping and exploiting a growing interest in Chinese and Japanese literature. Indeed, so far as actual range goes, the modern canon was essentially set down by the translators of the 1880s and 1890s. What they neglected or thought irrelevant – Lucretius, Tibullus, Latin poetry of the renaissance and baroque, the French neo-classics, the poetry of Goethe and Schiller – has not yet moved into the light. New renditions of Villon continue incessant when there are, as yet, hardly any of Maurice Scève, for instance, or Vigny. Pound broadened and gave critical orthodoxy to a body of values and emotional responses established by his pre-Raphaelite and Edwardian predecessors. What he revolutionized was the idiom of translation, the notion of what a translation is and of how it relates to the original.

Marianne Moore has summarized this revolution with her customary abruptness: 'the natural order of words, subject, predicate, object; the active voice where possible; a ban on dead words, rhymes synonymous with gusto.' These precepts stand for a whole vision of active re-statement. Pound's translations of Rihaku, Andreas Divus, Laforgue, Sophocles are re-enactments of the original poetic deed in the cadence, tonality, idiomatic stress of the modern. The translation exacts from the original the utmost of felt relevance; it carries to extreme Kierkegaard's dictum, 'It is not worth while remembering that past which cannot become a present'. In Pound's *mimesis*, Propertius and Cavalcanti 'become a present' so immediate to the ways we experience language and objectify emotion that the

Latin or Provençal poem is inseparable from the grammar of modernity. Pound's impact reaches far beyond the texts he himself has rendered; thus Ronald Knox's re-creation of the 'Lamentations of Jeremias' plainly reflects the rhythm and tone-colour of 'The Seafarer'.

But are these 'translations' by Pound and his numerous successors – Marianne Moore, Robert Lowell, Christopher Logue – translations in any proper sense? Or are they what Dryden terms *imitation*, 'where the translator (if he now has not lost that name) assumes the liberty not only to vary from the words and sense, but to forsake them both as he sees occasion; and taking only some general hints from the original, to run division on the ground-work, as he pleases'? A practice, adds Dryden, that is 'the greatest wrong which can be done to the memory and reputation of the dead'.

The quarrel over Pound's *Propertius* goes on (with recent argument suggesting that Pound's scholarship was not as hollow as professional Latinists would have it). Arrowsmith's treatment of Aristophanes and Robert Lowell's *Imitations* of Baudelaire or Pasternak pose it anew. It is, in part, a quarrel over semantics; the fact of radical change is no longer in doubt. The contemporary translator and even reader of classic verse comes after Pound as the modern painter comes after Cubism. Inevitably, much of the translation in this book implies and was made possible by Pound's enlargement of the term. I have taken translation to include *the writing of a poem in which a poem in another language (or in an earlier form of one's own language) is the vitalizing, shaping presence; a poem which can be read and responded to independently but which is not ontologically complete, a previous poem being its occasion, begetter, and in the literal sense, raison d'être.*

This is the definition implicit in the modern movement, in the extraordinary wealth and energy of verse translation, representation, imitation from Rossetti to George MacBeth. It cannot be rigorous; there are borderline cases which poet and reader play by ear. In this collection I have taken it to include Christopher Logue's ferocious re-statements of the *Iliad* – in which every modern line seems to me explicitly directed towards Homer's survivance, towards the presentment and 'presentness' of his songs – but to exclude Auden's 'Shield of Achilles' which is a commentary on, a critique from without of Homeric motifs. But the distinction can never be absolute.

Each poem in this book should have the original on the facing page. A prose paraphrase, perhaps bracketing the principal difficulties, should fill the margin as in a polyglot Bible. This is the only completely honest format for a reader and user of poetic translation. Obvious, though none the less obstructive reasons of size, economy, 'general appeal' have made this impossible. But this anthology would defeat itself if it did not, in whatever languages are accessible to him, return the reader to the original; if it did not direct him from the living mirror, however luminous, to the primary object. To *trans/late*: to carry over from what has been silent to what is vocal, from the distant to the near. But also to carry back.

GEORGE STEINER

ACKNOWLEDGEMENTS

My thanks go to friends and colleagues who have suggested poems they wanted included in such an anthology. I am grateful for the courtesy of the Cambridge University Library, and particularly to Mr P. J. Gautrey of the Anderson Room who met my numerous inquiries with unfailing kindness. Mr Anthony Richardson of Penguin Books has been a most generous supporter. But my principal indebtedness is to Elda Southern; her precision, quickness of eye and critical acumen have gone a long way toward making this book possible.

*

For permission to reprint poems in copyright, thanks are due to the following:
For HAROLD ACTON: to Curtis Brown Ltd for poems from *Modern Chinese Poetry*; for MARTIN S. ALLWOOD: to Andr. Fred Høst & Sons Forlag and Mr Martin Allwood for poems from *Modern Danish Poems* (ed. Knud K. Morgensen, 1949); for WILLIAM ARROWSMITH: to the University of Chicago Press for an extract from *The Bacchae*, copyright William Arrowsmith 1953, and to the University of Michigan Press for extracts from *The Birds*, copyright © William Arrowsmith 1961, and from *The Clouds*, copyright © William Arrowsmith 1962; for W. H. AUDEN: to Weidenfeld and Nicolson Ltd and Holt, Rinehart and Winston Inc. for a poem from *Half-Way to the Moon* (ed. Patricia Blake and Max Hayward), copyright © 1963 by Encounter Ltd; for MAURICE BARING: to the Baring Trustees for a poem from *Russian Lyrics*, published by William Heinemann Ltd; for ADRIAAN J. BARNOUW: to Rutgers University Press for a poem from *Coming After – An Anthology of Poetry from the Low Countries, 1948*; for SAMUEL BECKETT: to Mr Samuel Beckett for poems from *Eluard – Thorns of Thunder* (ed. George Reavey), published by Europa Press and Stanley Nott, 1937; for LAURENCE BINYON: to the Society of Authors as the literary representative of the Estate of the late Laurence Binyon for an extract from Dante's *Inferno*, translated by Laurence Binyon and published by Macmillan and Co. Ltd, 1933; for MAURICE BOWRA: to Macmillan and Co. Ltd for poems from *A Second Book of Russian Verse* (ed. Maurice Bowra); for NORMAN CAMERON: to the

Hogarth Press Ltd on behalf of the Estate of the late Norman Cameron for 'Poor People in Church' from *Arthur Rimbaud*, published by the Hogarth Press Ltd, 1942, and to Jonathan Cape Ltd for poems from *François Villon – Poems*, 1952; for ROY CAMPBELL: to Hughes Massey Ltd as the literary representatives of the Estate of the late Roy Campbell for poems from *Poems of Baudelaire* and *St John of the Cross*, both translated by Roy Campbell and published by the Harvill Press Ltd, 1952; to New Directions Publishing Corporation on behalf of the Estate of F. G. Lorca for poems from *Lorca – Collected Poems*, translated by Roy Campbell and published by New Directions, all rights reserved; to the Sylvan Press for poems from *Paco D'Arcos – Nostalgia*, translated by Roy Campbell, 1960; for G. K. CHESTERTON: to Miss D. E. Collins for a poem from *Collected Poems of G. K. Chesterton*, published by Burns, Oates and Washbourne Ltd, 1927 and to Dodd, Mead and Co., in whose edition of *The Collected Poems of G. K. Chesterton* (copyright 1932) the poem also appeared; for J. M. COHEN: to Mr J. M. Cohen and Ernest Benn Ltd for poems from *Boris Pasternak – Selected Poems*, translated by J. M. Cohen and published by Lindsay Drummond Ltd, 1946; for J. V. CUNNINGHAM: to Alan Swallow for extracts from *The Exclusions of a Rhyme: Poems and Epigrams*, published by Alan Swallow, copyright J. V. Cunningham 1960; for HILDA DOOLITTLE: to Grove Press Inc. for an extract from *H. D. – Selected Poems*, copyright 1957 Norman Holmes Pearson; for NATALIE DUDDINGTON: to Jonathan Cape Ltd for poems from *Forty-Seven Love Poems by Anna Akhmatova*, translated by Natalie Duddington and published by Jonathan Cape Ltd, 1927; for T. S. ELIOT: to Harcourt, Brace and World Inc. and Faber and Faber Ltd for an extract from *Anabasis* by Saint John Perce, translated by T. S. Eliot, copyright 1938–9 by Harcourt, Brace and World Inc.; for *William Empson:* to Professor Empson for 'Chinese Peasant Song', which appeared in *Nine*, Autumn 1952, to Chatto and Windus Ltd, publishers of *Collected Poems of William Empson* and to Harcourt, Brace and World Inc., publishers of *Collected Poems* by William Empson, copyright, 1935, 1940, 1949 by William Empson; for D. J. ENRIGHT: to John Murray Ltd for a poem from *The Poetry of Living Japan* by D. J. Enright, 1957; for DUDLEY FITTS: to Faber and Faber Ltd and New

Directions for poems from *From The Greek Anthology* by Dudley Fitts, copyright 1938, 1941, © 1956 by New Directions; for DUDLEY FITTS and ROBERT FITZGERALD: to Harcourt, Brace and World Inc. for an extract from *Antigone: An English Version* by Dudley Fitts and Robert Fitzgerald, copyright 1939 by Harcourt, Brace and World Inc.; for Robert Fitzgerald to New Directions for an extract from *In The Rose Of Our Time*, copyright 1956 by Robert Fitzgerald; to William Heinemann Ltd and Doubleday and Co. Inc. for extracts from *The Odyssey*, copyright © 1961 by Robert Fitzgerald; for SCOTT FITZGERALD: to Weidenfeld and Nicolson Ltd and Viking Press Inc. for 'Voyelles' from *College of One* by Sheilah Graham (all rights reserved); for G. S. FRASER: to Mr Fraser and the editors of *Nine* (Winter, 1949); for J. GRADISNIK: to Calder and Boyars Ltd for a poem from *Anthology of Modern Yugoslav Poetry* (ed. Janko Lavrin), published by John Calder Ltd, 1962; for HORACE GREGORY: to Grove Press Inc. for poems from *The Poems of Catullus*, copyright © 1956 Horace Gregory; for MICHAEL HAMBURGER and CHRISTOPHER MIDDLETON: to MacGibbon and Kee Ltd for poems from *Modern German Poetry*, 1962; for MICHAEL HAMBURGER: to Mr Michael Hamburger for 'Grodek' from *Decline*, published by Guido Morris, 1952; for THOMAS HARDY: to Macmillan and Co. Ltd and the Macmillan Company of America for poems from *The Collected Poems of Thomas Hardy*, 1930; for HENRY HART: to Stanford University Press for an extract from *Poems of the Hundred Names* by Henry H. Hart, copyright 1933, 1938 by the Regents of the University of California, 1954 by the Board of Trustees of the Leland Stanford Junior University; for JOHN HEATH STUBBS: to David Higham Associates Ltd for 'To Himself' from *Poems of Giacomo Leopardi*, published by Oxford University Press, and to the New American Library Inc., publishers of *Giacomo Leopardi — Selected Poetry and Prose*, in which the poem also appears; for BRIAN HILL: to Rupert Hart-Davis Ltd for poems from *The Drunken Boat — 36 Poems by Rimbaud*, translated by Brian Hill, 1952; for GERARD MANLEY HOPKINS: to Oxford University Press for poems from *Poems of Gerard Manley Hopkins* (ed. W. H. Gardner and Geoffrey Cumberledge), 1952; for A. E. HOUSMAN: to the Society of Authors as the literary representative of the Estate of the late A. E. Housman and to Messrs Jonathan Cape Ltd for poems from *A. E. Housman – Collected Poems*, published by Jonathan Cape Ltd, 1939; for JAMES JOYCE: to the Society of Authors as the literary representative of the Estate of the late James Joyce; for EDMUND KEELEY: to the Modern Poetry Association for poems from *Poetry* (October 1964); for EDMUND KEELEY and PHILIP SHERRARD: to Thames and Hudson Ltd for poems from *Six Poets of Modern Greece* (ed. Edmund Keeley and Philip Sherrard), 1960; for DONALD KEENE: to Thames and Hudson Ltd and Grove Press Inc. for a poem from *Modern Japanese Literature* (compiled and edited by Donald Keene), copyright © 1956 by Grove Press; for RUDYARD KIPLING: to Mrs George Bambridge, Macmillan and Co. Ltd, and the Macmillan Company of Canada Ltd for a poem from *A Diversity of Creatures* and to Doubleday and Co. Inc., publishers of *Rudyard Kipling's Verse: Definitive Edition*, in which the poem also appears; for RONALD KNOX: to His Eminence, the Cardinal Archbishop of Westminster for an extract from *The Old Testament, Volume II* in the translation of Monsignor Ronald Knox, copyright 1950, Sheed and Ward Inc., New York, and to Burns and Oates Ltd, publishers of *The Bible*, translated by Monsignor Ronald Knox, in which the extract also appears; for S. KUNITZ: to Weidenfeld and Nicolson Ltd and Holt, Rinehart and Winston Inc. for a poem from *Half-Way to the Moon* (ed. Patricia Blake and Max Hayward), copyright © 1963 by Encounter Ltd; for RICHMOND LATTIMORE: to the University of Chicago Press for extracts from *Greek Lyrics*, *Aeschylus – Agamemnon*, Volume I, and *Euripides – Helen*; for Peter Lee: to the John Day Co. Inc. for poems from *Anthology of Korean Poetry* by Peter H. Lee, copyright © 1964 by UNESCO; for J. B. LEISHMAN: to Bruno Cassirer Ltd for an extract from *Translating Horace* by J. B. Leishman, 1956; for C. DAY LEWIS: to the Hogarth Press for an extract from Mr C. Day Lewis's translation of the *Aeneid* of Virgil, 1954; for CHRISTOPHER LOGUE: to Hutchinson and Co. Ltd and Ivan Obolensky Inc. for two translations of poems by Neruda from *Songs* by Christopher Logue, copyright Christopher Logue, 1959; to the Scorpion Press for an extract from *Patrocleia* by Christopher Logue, 1962; for ROBERT LOWELL: to Faber and Faber Ltd and Farrar, Straus and Giroux Inc. for poems from *Imitations*, copyright © 1958, 1959, 1960, 1961 by

Robert Lowell; for GEORGE MACBETH: to the Scorpion Press for a poem from *A Doomsday Book*, 1965; for LOUIS MACNEICE: to Faber and Faber Ltd and Harcourt, Brace and World Inc. for an extract from *The Agamemnon of Aeschylus*, translated by Louis MacNeice; for EDWARD MARSH: to Macmillan and Co. Ltd for an extract from *Horace Odes*, translated by Edward Marsh, 1941; for JOHN MASEFIELD: to the Society of Authors, Dr John Masefield O.M. and The Macmillan Company of America for 'I Saw the Ramparts' from *The Story of a Round House* by John Masefield, copyright 1912 The Macmillan Company, renewed 1940 by John Masefield; for KENNETH MCROBBIE: to Peter Owen Ltd for extracts from *The Plough and the Pen: Writings from Hungary*, 1963; for W. S. MERWIN: to Abelard-Schuman Ltd and Doubleday and Co Inc. for poems from *Spanish Ballads* (ed. W. S. Merwin), copyright © 1961 by W. S. Merwin; for JAMES MICHIE: to Rupert Hart-Davis Ltd for extracts from *The Odes of Horace*, translated by James Michie, 1964; for CZESŁAW MIŁOSZ: to Doubleday and Co. Inc. for poems from *Postwar Polish Poetry* (ed. Czesław Miłosz), copyright © 1965 by Czesław Miłosz; for J. K. MONTGOMERY and EWALD OSERS: to Dilia, Czechoslovakia, on behalf of the authors' heirs and the translators for poems from *Modern Czech Poetry*, published by the Prague Press; for MARIANNE MOORE: to the Viking Press Inc. for poems from *The Marianne Moore Reader* by Marianne Moore, copyright © 1952, 1954 by Marianne Moore and for 'The Cat and the Rat' from *The Fables of La Fontaine* by Marianne Moore, copyright © 1954 by Marianne Moore; for GILBERT MURRAY: to Allen and Unwin Ltd for extracts from *Athenian Drama – Euripides* and *Sophocles – Antigone* by Gilbert Murray; for VLADIMIR NABOKOV: to Weidenfeld and Nicolson Ltd and Alfred A. Knopf Inc. for an extract from *The Song of Igor's Campaign*, 1960; for FRANK O'CONNOR: to A. D. Peters and Co. for poems from *Kings, Lords and Commons*, copyright Frank O'Connor 1961; for EZRA POUND: to Harvard University Press for 'Airs from the Book of Odes', from *The Classic Anthology Defined by Confucius*, copyright 1954 by the President and Fellows of Harvard College; to Neville Spearman Ltd for extracts from *Women of Trachis*, 1956; to Mr A. V. Moore and New Directions for poems from *Translations*, copyright 1926, 1954, 1963 by Ezra Pound, *Personae*, copyright 1926, 1954 by Ezra Pound, and *The Cantos*, copyright 1934, 1948 by Ezra Pound; for SIMON RAVEN: to Lady Storrs for an extract from *Ad Pyrrham* (ed. Ronald Storrs), published by Oxford University Press, 1959; for GEORGE REAVEY: to Weidenfeld and Nicolson Ltd and the World Publishing Company for a poem from *The Bedbug and Selected Poetry* by George Reavey, 1961; for KENNETH REXROTH: to the University of Michigan Press for poems from *From The Greek Anthology* by Kenneth Rexroth, copyright © 1962 by the University of Michigan; for GEORGE SANTAYANA: to Charles Scribner's Sons for extracts from *A Hermit of Carmel and Other Poems* by George Santayana, copyright Charles Scribner's Sons 1901 and to Constable and Co. Ltd, publishers of *George Santayana: Poems*, 1922, in which the poems also appear; for BURNS SINGER: to Secker and Warburg Ltd for poems from *Five Centuries of Polish Poetry* by Burns Singer (with Jerzy Peterkiewiez), 1960; for STEPHEN SPENDER: to the Hogarth Press Ltd for 'Lament for Ignacio Sanchez Mejias' from *Selected Poems of Federico Garcia Lorca* by Stephen Spender (with J. L. Gili) 1943, and to the Trianon Press for 'From the Depth of the Abyss' from the French of Eluard by Stephen Spender in *Dur Desir de Dürer*; for A. C. SWINBURNE: to William Heinemann Ltd for 'Epitaph in the form of a Ballad' from *A. C. Swinburne – Collected Poetical Works*, Volume I, 1924; to Syracuse University Press for 'Ballad of Villon and Fat Madge' from *New Writings of Swinburne* (ed. C. Lang), 1965; for A. J. SYMONS: to Secker and Warburg Ltd for poems from *A. J. Symons – Collected Poems*, 1924; for NATHANIEL TARN: to Jonathan Cape Ltd for a poem from *Pablo Neruda* by Nathaniel Tarn; for ALLEN TATE: to Eyre and Spottiswoode Ltd and Charles Scribner's Sons for a poem from *Allen Tate: Poems*, copyright 1931, 1932, 1937, 1948 Charles Scribner's Sons; renewal copyright © 1959, 1960 Allen Tate; for HELEN WADDELL: to Constable and Co. Ltd for poems from *Mediaeval Latin Lyrics* 1948; for ARTHUR WALEY: to Allen and Unwin Ltd for poems from *Chinese Poems*, *The Poetry and Career of Li Po*, and *The Temple and Other Poems*; to Constable and Co. Ltd for 'Seventeen Old Poems', 'On the Birth of his Son', 'The Red Hills', 'The Charcoal-Seller', 'To His Wife', and 'The Scholar in the Narrow Street' from *170 Chinese Poems*; for VERNON WATKINS: to Faber and Faber Ltd for a poem from

ACKNOWLEDGEMENTS

Heinrich Heine by Vernon Watkins, 1955; for THEODOOR WEEVERS: to the Athlone Press, University of London, for a poem from *Poetry of the Netherlands in its European Context* by Theodoor Weevers, 1960; for RICHARD WILBUR to Weidenfeld and Nicolson Ltd and Holt, Rinehart and Winston Inc. for 'Anti-Worlds' from *Half-Way to the Moon* (ed. Patricia Blake and Max Hayward), copyright © 1963 by Encounter Ltd; to Faber and Faber Ltd and Harcourt, Brace and World Inc. for 'The Agrigentum Road' from *Advice to a Prophet and Other Poems*, copyright © 1961 by Richard Wilbur, for an extract from *Molière – Tartuffe*, copyright © 1962, 1963 by Richard Wilbur, and for 'Francis Jammes – A Prayer' and 'Paul Valéry – Helen' from *Things of This World*, copyright © 1956 by Richard Wilbur; for W. B. YEATS: to Macmillan and Co. Ltd, publishers of *The Collected Poems of W. B. Yeats*, and to The Macmillan Company of America for 'At the Abbey Theatre' from *The Green Helmet and Other Poems* by William Butler Yeats, copyright 1912 The Macmillan Company, renewed 1940 by Bertha Georgie Yeats; for 'When You Are Old' from *Poetic Works* by William Butler Yeats, copyright 1906 The Macmillan Company, renewed 1934 by William B. Yeats; for 'Colonus Praise' from *The Tower* by William Butler Yeats, copyright The Macmillan Company 1928, renewed 1956 by Bertha Georgie Yeats; and for 'From the Antigone' from *The Winding Stair* by William Butler Yeats, copyright The Macmillan Company 1933, renewed 1961 by Bertha Georgie Yeats.

Every effort has been made to trace copyright holders, but in a few cases this has proved impossible. The publishers would be interested to hear from any copyright holders not here acknowledged.

WILLIAM EWART GLADSTONE
(1809–1898)

FROM THE LATIN OF HORACE

An Epilogue

(*Odes*, Book III, 30) .

Now have I reared a monument
      more durable than brass,
And one that doth the royal scale
      of pyramids surpass,
Nor shall defeated Aquilo
      destroy, nor soaking rain,
Nor yet the countless tide of years,
      nor seasons in their train.
Not all of me shall die: my praise
      shall grow, and never end,
While pontiff and mute vestal shall
      the Capitol ascend,
And so a mighty share of me
      shall Libitina foil.
Where bellows headstrong Aufidus,
      where, on his arid soil,
King Daunus ruled a rural folk,
      of me it shall be told
That, grown from small to great, I first
      of all men subtly wrought
Aeolian strains to unison
      with our Italian thought.
So take thine honours earned by deeds;
      and graciously do thou,
Melpomenè, with Delphic bays
      adorn thy poet's brow.

DANTE GABRIEL ROSSETTI
(1828–1882)

Sonnet: To the Guelf Faction

Because ye made your backs your shields, it came
  To pass, ye Guelfs, that these your enemies
  From hares grew lions: and because your eyes
Turn'd homeward, and your spurs e'en did the same,
Full many an one who still might win the game
  In fever'd tracts of exile pines and dies.
  Ye blew your bubbles as the falcon flies,
And the wind broke them up and scatter'd them.
This counsel, therefore. Shape your high resolves
  In good King Robert's humour, and afresh
    Accept your shames, forgive, and go your way,
  And so her peace is made with Pisa! Yea,
  What cares she for the miserable flesh
That in the wilderness has fed the wolves?

Sestina
Of the Lady Pietra degli Scrovigni

To the dim light and the large circle of shade
I have clomb, and to the whitening of the hills,
There where we see no colour in the grass.
Nathless my longing loses not its green,
It has so taken root in the hard stone
Which talks and hears as though it were a lady.

Utterly frozen is this youthful lady,
Even as the snow that lies within the shade;
For she is no more moved than is a stone
By the sweet season which makes warm the hills

And alters them afresh from white to green,
Covering their sides again with flowers and grass.

When on her hair she sets a crown of grass
The thought has no more room for other lady;
Because she weaves the yellow with the green
So well that Love sits down there in the shade, –
Love who has shut me in among low hills
Faster than between walls of granite-stone.

She is more bright than is a precious stone;
The wound she gives may not be heal'd with grass:
I therefore have fled far o'er plains and hills
For refuge from so dangerous a lady;
But from her sunshine nothing can give shade, –
Not any hill, nor wall, nor summer-green.

A while ago, I saw her dress'd in green, –
So fair, she might have waken'd in a stone
This love which I do feel even for her shade;
And therefore, as one woos a graceful lady,
I wooed her in a field that was all grass
Girdled about with very lofty hills.

Yet shall the streams turn back and climb the hills
Before Love's flame in this damp wood and green
Burn, as it burns within a youthful lady,
For my sake, who would sleep away in stone
My life, or feed like beasts upon the grass,
Only to see her garments cast a shade.

How dark soe'er the hills throw out their shade,
Under her summer-green the beautiful lady
Covers it, like a stone cover'd in grass.

FROM THE ITALIAN OF GUIDO CAVALCANTI

I

Sonnet: A Rapture Concerning his Lady

Who is she coming, whom all gaze upon,
Who makes the air all tremulous with light,

And at whose side is Love himself? that none
  Dare speak, but each man's sighs are infinite.
    Ah me! how she looks round from left to right,
Let Love discourse: I may not speak thereon.
Lady she seems of such high benison
  As makes all others graceless in men's sight.
The honour which is hers cannot be said;
  To whom are subject all things virtuous,
    While all things beauteous own her deity.
Ne'er was the mind of man so nobly led,
  Nor yet was such redemption granted us
    That we should ever know her perfectly.

2

Ballata: Of a Continual Death in Love

Though thou, indeed, hast quite forgotten ruth,
Its steadfast truth my heart abandons not;
But still its thought yields service in good part
    To that hard heart in thee.

Alas! who hears believes not I am so.
Yet who can know? of very surety, none.
From Love is won a spirit, in some wise,
    Which dies perpetually:

And, when at length in that strange ecstasy
    The heavy sigh will start,
    There rains upon my heart
    A love so pure and fine,
That I say: 'Lady, I am wholly thine.'

WILLIAM MORRIS
(1834–1896)

FROM THE LATIN OF VIRGIL

The Sleep of Palinurus

(*Aeneid*, Book v, lines 847–871)

But Palinure with scarce-raised eyes e'en such an answer gave:
'To gentle countenance of sea and quiet of the wave
Deem'st thou me dull? would'st have me trow in such a monster's
    truth?
And shall I mine Aeneas trust to lying breeze forsooth,
I, fool of peaceful heaven and sea so many times of old?'

So saying to the helm he clung, nor ever left his hold,
And all the while the stars above his eyen toward them drew.
But lo, the God brought forth a bough wet with Lethean dew,
And sleepy with the might of Styx, and shook it therewithal
Over his brow, and loosed his lids delaying still to fall:
But scarce in first of stealthy sleep his limbs all loosened lay,
When, weighing on him, did he tear a space of stern away,
And rolled him, helm and wrack and all, into the flowing wave
Headlong, and crying oft in vain for fellowship to save:
Then Sleep himself amid thin air flew, borne upon the wing.

No less the ship-host sails the sea, its safe way following
Untroubled 'neath the plighted word of Father Neptune's mouth.
So to the Sirens' rocks they draw, a dangerous pass forsooth
In yore agone, now white with bones of many a perished man.
Thence ever roared the salt sea now as on the rocks it ran;
And there the Father felt the ship fare wild and fitfully,
Her helmsman lost; so he himself steered o'er the night-tide sea,
Sore weeping; for his fellow's end his inmost heart did touch:
'O Palinure, that trowed the sky and soft seas overmuch,
Now naked on an unknown shore thy resting-place shall be!'

ALGERNON CHARLES SWINBURNE

(1837–1909)

FROM THE FRENCH OF FRANÇOIS VILLON

I

The Ballad of Villon and Fat Madge

''Tis no sin for a man to labour in his vocation.'
'The night cometh, when no man can work.'

What though the beauty I love and serve be cheap,
    Ought you to take me for a beast or fool?
All things a man could wish are in her keep;
    For her I turn swashbuckler in love's school.
    When folk drop in, I take my pot and stool
And fall to drinking with no more ado.
I fetch them bread, fruit, cheese, and water, too;
    I say all's right so long as I'm well paid;
'Look in again when your flesh troubles you,
    Inside this brothel where we drive our trade.'

But soon the devil's among us flesh and fell,
    When penniless to bed comes Madge my whore;
I loathe the very sight of her like hell.
    I snatch gown, girdle, surcoat, all she wore,
    And tell her, these shall stand against her score.
She grips her hips with both hands, cursing God,
Swearing by Jesus' body, bones, and blood,
    That they shall not. Then I, no whit dismayed,
Cross her cracked nose with some stray shiver of wood
    Inside this brothel where we drive our trade.

When all's up she drops me a windy word,
    Bloat like a beetle puffed and poisonous:
Grins, thumps my pate, and calls me dickey-bird,
    And cuffs me with a fist that's ponderous.
    We sleep like logs, being drunken both of us;

Then when we wake her womb begins to stir;
To save her seed she gets me under her
   Wheezing and whining, flat as planks are laid:
And thus she spoils me for a whoremonger
   Inside this brothel where we drive our trade.

Blow, hail or freeze, I've bread here baked rent free!
Whoring's my trade, and my whore pleases me;
   Bad cat, bad rat; we're just the same if weighed.
We that love filth, filth follows us, you see;
Honour flies from us, as from her we flee
   Inside this brothel where we drive our trade.*

    * I bequeath likewise to fat Madge
      This little song to learn and study;
    By God's head she's a sweet fat fadge,
      Devout and soft of flesh and ruddy;
    I love her with my soul and body,
    So doth she me, sweet dainty thing.
      If you fall in with such a lady,
    Read it, and give it her to sing.

2

The Epitaph in Form of a Ballad

(Which Villon made for himself and his comrades, expecting
to be hanged along with them)

Men, brother men, that after us yet live,
   Let not your hearts too hard against us be;
For if some pity of us poor men ye give,
   The sooner God shall take of you pity.
   Here are we five or six strung up, you see,
And here the flesh that all too well we fed
Bit by bit eaten and rotten, rent and shred,
   And we the bones grow dust and ash withal;
Let no man laugh at us discomforted,
   But pray to God that he forgive us all.

If we call on you, brothers, to forgive,
   Ye should not hold our prayer in scorn, though we

Were slain by law; ye know that all alive
   Have not wit always to walk righteously;
   Make therefore intercession heartily
With him that of a virgin's womb was bred,
That his grace be not as a dry well-head
   For us, nor let hell's thunder on us fall;
We are dead, let no man harry or vex us dead,
   But pray to God that he forgive us all.

The rain has washed and laundered us all five,
   And the sun dried and blackened; yea, perdie,
Ravens and pies with beaks that rend and rive
   Have dug our eyes out, and plucked off for fee
   Our beards and eyebrows; never are we free,
Not once, to rest; but here and there still sped,
Drive at its wild will by the wind's change led,
   More pecked of birds than fruits on garden-wall;
Men, for God's love, let no gibe here be said,
   But pray to God that he forgive us all.

Prince Jesus, that of all art Lord and head,
Keep us, that hell be not our bitter bed;
   We have nought to do in such a master's hall.
Be not ye therefore of our fellowhead,
   But pray to God that he forgive us all.

THOMAS HARDY
(1840–1928)

Sapphic Fragment

'Thou shalt be – Nothing.' – OMAR KHAYYAM
'Tombless, with no remembrance.' – SHAKESPEARE

> Dead shalt thou lie; and nought
> Be told of thee or thought,
> For thou hast plucked not of the Muses' tree:
> And even in Hades' halls
> Amidst thy fellow-thralls
> No friendly shade thy shade shall company!

FROM THE LATIN OF CATULLUS

XXXI : Sirmio

(After passing Sirmione, April 1887)

Sirmio, thou dearest dear of strands
That Neptune strokes in lake and sea,
With what high joy from stranger lands
Doth thy old friend set foot on thee!
Yea, barely seems it true to me
That no Bithynia holds me now,
But calmly and assuringly
Around me stretchest homely Thou.

Is there a scene more sweet than when
Our clinging cares are undercast,
And, worn by alien moils and men,
The long untrodden sill repassed,
We press the pined for couch at last,
And find a full repayment there?
Then hail, sweet Sirmio; thou that wast,
And art, mine own unrivalled Fair!

GERARD MANLEY HOPKINS
(1844–1889)

FROM THE LATIN OF HORACE

1

Persicos odi, puer, apparatus

(*Odes*, Book I, 38)

Ah child, no Persian – perfect art!
Crowns composite and braided bast
They tease me. Never know the part
    Where roses linger last.

Bring natural myrtle, and have done:
Myrtle will suit your place and mine:
And set the glasses from the sun
    Beneath the tackled vine.

2

Odi profanum volgus et arceo

(*Odes*, Book III, 1)

Tread back – and back, the lewd and lay! –
Grace guard your tongues! – what never ear
Heard yet, the Muses' man, today
I bid the boys and maidens hear.

Kings herd it on their subject droves
But Jove's the herd that keeps the kings –
Jove of the Giants: simple Jove's
Mere eyebrow rocks this round of things.

Say man than man may more enclose
In rankèd vineyards; one with claim
Of blood to our green hustings goes;
One with more conscience, cleaner fame;

54

One better backed comes crowding by: —
That level power whose word is Must
Dances the balls for low or high:
Her urn takes all, her deal is just.

Sinner who saw the blade that hung
Vertical home, could Sicily fare
Be managed tasty to that tongue?
Or bird with pipe, viol with air

Bring sleep round then? — sleep not afraid
Of country bidder's calls or low
Entries or banks all over shade
And Tempe with the west to blow.

Who stops his asking mood at par
The burly sea may quite forget
Nor fear the violent calendar
At Haedus-rise, Arcturus-set,

For hail upon the vine nor break
His heart at farming, what between
The dog-star with the fields abake
And spitting snows to choke the green.

Fish feel their waters drawing to
With our abutments: there we see
The lades discharged and laded new,
And Italy flies from Italy.

But fears, fore-motions of the mind,
Climb quits: one boards the master there
On brazèd barge and hard behind
Sits to the beast that seats him — Care.

O if there's that which Phrygian stone
And crimson wear of starry shot
Not sleek away; Falernian-grown
And oils of Shushan comfort not,

Why .   .   .   .   .   .
.   .   .   .   .   .   *
Why should I change a Sabine dale
For wealth as wide as weariness?

*Hopkins left this translation incomplete

LADY AUGUSTA GREGORY
(1859–1932)

FROM THE IRISH (ANON.)

Donall Oge: Grief of a Girl's Heart

O Donall oge, if you go across the sea,
Bring myself with you and do not forget it;
And you will have a sweetheart for fair days and market days,
And the daughter of the King of Greece beside you at night.

It is late last night the dog was speaking of you;
The snipe was speaking of you in her deep marsh.
It is you are the lonely bird through the woods;
And that you may be without a mate until you find me.

You promised me, and you said a lie to me,
That you would be before me where the sheep are flocked;
I gave a whistle and three hundred cries to you,
And I found nothing there but a bleating lamb.

You promised me a thing that was hard for you,
A ship of gold under a silver mast;
Twelve towns with a market in all of them,
And a fine white court by the side of the sea.

You promised me a thing that is not possible,
That you would give me gloves of the skin of a fish;
That you would give me shoes of the skin of a bird;
And a suit of the dearest silk in Ireland.

O Donall oge, it is I would be better to you
Than a high, proud, spendthrift lady:
I would milk the cow; I would bring help to you;
And if you were hard pressed, I would strike a blow for you.

O, ochone, and it's not with hunger
Or with wanting food, or drink, or sleep,
That I am growing thin, and my life is shortened;
But it is the love of a young man has withered me away.

It is early in the morning that I saw him coming,
Going along the road on the back of a horse;
He did not come to me; he made nothing of me;
And it is on my way home that I cried my fill.

When I go by myself to the Well of Loneliness,
I sit down and I go through my trouble;
When I see the world and do not see my boy,
He that has an amber shade in his hair.

It was on that Sunday I gave my love to you;
The Sunday that is last before Easter Sunday.
And myself on my knees reading the Passion;
And my two eyes giving love to you for ever.

O, aya! my mother, give myself to him;
And give him all that you have in the world;
Get out yourself to ask for alms,
And do not come back and forward looking for me.

My mother said to me not to be talking with you today,
Or tomorrow, or on Sunday;
It was a bad time she took for telling me that;
It was shutting the door after the house was robbed.

My heart is as black as the blackness of the sloe,
Or as the black coal that is on the smith's forge;
Or as the sole of a shoe left in white halls;
It was you put that darkness over my life.

You have taken the east from me; You have taken the west from
    me
You have taken what is before me and what is behind me;
You have taken the moon, you have taken the sun from me,
And my fear is great that you have taken God from me!

ALFRED EDWARD HOUSMAN
(1859–1936)

FROM THE LATIN OF HORACE

Diffugere Nives

(*Odes*, Book IV, 7)

The snows are fled away, leaves on the shaws
    And grasses in the mead renew their birth,
The river to the river-bed withdraws,
    And altered is the fashion of the earth.

The Nymphs and Graces three put off their fear
    And unapparelled in the woodland play.
The swift hour and the brief prime of the year
    Say to the soul, *Thou wast not born for aye.*

Thaw follows frost; hard on the heel of spring
    Treads summer sure to die, for hard on hers
Comes autumn, with his apples scattering;
    Then back to wintertide, when nothing stirs.

But oh, whate'er the sky-led seasons mar,
    Moon upon moon rebuilds it with her beams:
Come *we* where Tullus and where Ancus are,
    And good Aeneas, we are dust and dreams.

Torquatus, if the gods in heaven shall add
    The morrow to the day, what tongue has told?
Feast then thy heart, for what thy heart has had
    The fingers of no heir will ever hold.

When thou descendest once the shades among,
    The stern assize and equal judgment o'er,
Not thy long lineage nor thy golden tongue,
    No, nor thy righteousness, shall friend thee more.

Night holds Hippolytus the pure of stain,
    Diana steads him nothing, he must stay;

And Theseus leaves Pirithöus in the chain
  The love of comrades cannot take away.

FROM THE GREEK OF SOPHOCLES

2

Oedipus Coloneus

(lines 1211–1248)

What man is he that yearneth
  For length unmeasured of days?
Folly mine eye discerneth
  Encompassing all his ways.
For years over-running the measure
  Shall change thee in evil wise:
Grief draweth nigh thee; and pleasure,
  Behold, it is hid from thine eyes.
  This to their wage have they
  Which overlive their day.
And He that looseth from labour
  Doth one with other befriend,
  Whom bride nor bridesmen attend,
Song, nor sound of the tabor,
  Death, that maketh an end.

Thy portion esteem I highest,
  Who wast not ever begot;
Thine next, being born who diest
  And straightway again art not.
With follies light as the feather
  Doth Youth to man befall;
Then evils gather together,
  There wants not one of them all –
  Wrath, envy, discord, strife,
  The sword that seeketh life.
And sealing the sum of trouble
  Doth tottering Age draw nigh,
  Whom friends and kinsfolk fly,

Age, upon whom redouble
   All sorrows under the sky.

This man, as me, even so,
Have the evil days overtaken;
And like as a cape sea-shaken
With tempest at earth's last verges
And shock of all winds that blow,
His head the seas of woe,
The thunders of awful surges
Ruining overflow;
Blown from the fall of even,
   Blown from the dayspring forth,
Blown from the noon in heaven,
   Blown from night and the North.

GEORGE SANTAYANA
(1863–1952)

FROM THE ITALIAN OF MICHELANGELO

'Gli occhi miei vaghi delle cose belle'

Ravished by all that to the eyes is fair,
Yet hungry for the joys that truly bless,
My soul can find no stair
To mount to heaven, save earth's loveliness.
For from the stars above
Descends a glorious light
That lifts our longing to their highest height
And bears the name of love.
Nor is there aught can move
A gentle heart, or purge or make it wise,
But beauty and the starlight of her eyes.

FROM THE FRENCH OF THÉOPHILE GAUTIER

Art

All things are doubly fair
If patience fashion them
    And care –
Verse, enamel, marble, gem.

No idle chains endure:
Yet, Muse, to walk aright,
    Lace tight
Thy buskin proud and sure.

Fie on a facile measure,
A shoe where every lout
    At pleasure
Slips his foot in and out!

Sculptor, lay by the clay
On which thy nerveless finger
    May linger,
Thy thoughts flown far away.

Keep to Carrara rare,
Struggle with Paros cold,
    That hold
The subtle line and fair.

Lest haply nature lose
That proud, that perfect line,
    Make thine
The bronze of Syracuse.

And with a tender dread
Upon an agate's face
    Retrace
Apollo's golden head.

Despise a watery hue
And tints that soon expire.
    With fire
Burn thine enamel true.

Twine, twine in artful wise
The blue-green mermaid's arms,
   · Mid charms
Of thousand heraldries.

Show in their triple lobe
Virgin and Child, that hold
    Their globe,
Cross-crowned and aureoled.

– All things return to dust
Save beauties fashioned well.
    The bust
Outlasts the citadel.

Oft doth the ploughman's heel,
Breaking an ancient clod,
    Reveal
A Caesar or a god.

The gods, too, die, alas!
But deathless and more strong
      Than brass
Remains the sovereign song.

Chisel and carve and file,
Till thy vague dream imprint
      Its smile
On the unyielding flint.

RUDYARD KIPLING
(1865–1936)

HORACE, BOOK V, ODE 3*
A Translation

There are whose study is of smells,
    And to attentive schools rehearse
How something mixed with something else
    Makes something worse.

Some cultivate in broths impure
    The clients of our body – these,
Increasing without Venus, cure,
    Or cause, disease.

Others the heated wheel extol,
    And all its offspring, whose concern
Is how to make it farthest roll
    And fastest turn.

Me, much incurious if the hour
    Present, or to be paid for, brings
Me to Brundusium by the power
    Of wheels or wings;

Me, in whose breast no flame hath burned
    Life-long, save that by Pindar lit,
Such lore leaves cold. I am not turned
    Aside to it

More than when, sunk in thought profound
    Of what the unaltering Gods require,
My steward (friend but slave) brings round
    Logs for my fire.

* The Latin 'original' of this *Translation* is not, of course, easy to locate.

ARTHUR SYMONS
(1865–1945)

1

Clair de Lune

Your soul is a sealed garden, and there go
With masque and bergamasque fair companies
Playing on lutes and dancing and as though
Sad under their fantastic fripperies.

Though they in minor keys go carolling
Of love the conqueror and of life the boon
They seem to doubt the happiness they sing
And the song melts into the light of the moon,

The sad light of the moon, so lovely fair
That all the birds dream in the leafy shade
And the slim fountains sob into the air
Among the marble statues in the glade.

2

Femme et Chatte

They were at play, she and her cat,
And it was marvellous to mark
The white paws and the white hand pat
Each other in the deepening dark.

The stealthy little lady hid
Under her mittens' silken sheath
Her deadly agate nails that thrid
The silk-like dagger-points of death.

The cat purred primly and drew in

Her claws that were of steel filed thin:
The devil was in it all the same.

And in the boudoir, while a shout
Of laughter in the air rang out,
Four sparks of phosphor shone like flame.

3

O Mon Dieu

O my God, Thou hast wounded me with love,
Behold the wound, that is still vibrating,
O my God, Thou hast wounded me with love.

O my God, Thy fear hath fallen upon me,
Behold the burn is there, and it throbs aloud,
O my God, Thy fear hath fallen upon me.

O my God, I have known that all is vile
And that Thy glory hath stationed itself in me,
O my God, I have known that all is vile.

Drown my soul in floods, floods of Thy wine,
Mingle my life with body of Thy bread,
Drown my soul in floods, floods of Thy wine.

Take my blood, that I have not poured out,
Take my flesh, unworthy of suffering,
Take my blood, that I have not poured out.

Take my brow, that has only learned to blush,
To be the footstool of Thine adorable feet,
Take my brow, that has only learned to blush.

Take my hands, because they have laboured not
For coals of fire and for rare frankincense,
Take my hands, because they have laboured not.

Take my heart, that has beaten for vain things,
To throb under the thorns of Calvary,
Take my heart, that has beaten for vain things.

Take my feet, frivolous travellers,
That they may run to the crying of Thy grace,
Take my feet, frivolous travellers.

Take my voice, a harsh and a lying noise,
For the reproaches of Thy Penitence,
Take my voice, a harsh and a lying noise.

Take mine eyes, luminaries of deceit,
That they may be extinguished in the tears of prayer,
Take mine eyes, luminaries of deceit.

Alas, Thou, God of pardon and promises,
What is the pit of mine ingratitude,
Alas, Thou, God of pardon and promises.

God of terror and God of holiness,
Alas, my sinfulness is a black abyss,
God of terror and God of holiness.

Thou, God of peace, of joy and delight,
All my tears, all my ignorances,
Thou, God of peace, of joy and delight.

Thou, O God, knowest all this, all this,
How poor I am, poorer than any man,
Thou, O God, knowest all this, all this.

And what I have, my God, I give to Thee.

FROM THE LATIN OF CATULLUS

Lesbia

Caelius, Lesbia mine, that Lesbia, that
Lesbia whom Catullus for love did rate
Higher than all himself and than all things, stands
Now at the cross-roads and the alleys, to wait
From the lords of Rome, with public lips and hands.

WILLIAM BUTLER YEATS
(1865–1939)

I

'When you are old . . .'

When you are old and grey and full of sleep,
And nodding by the fire, take down this book,
And slowly read, and dream of the soft look
Your eyes had once, and of their shadows deep;

How many loved your moments of glad grace,
And loved your beauty with love false or true,
But one man loved the pilgrim soul in you,
And loved the sorrows of your changing face;

And bending down beside the glowing bars,
Murmur, a little sadly, how Love fled
And paced upon the mountains overhead
And hid his face amid a crowd of stars.

2

At the Abbey Theatre

(Imitated from Ronsard)

Dear Craoibhin Aoibhin, look into our case.
When we are high and airy hundreds say
That if we hold that flight they'll leave the place,
While those same hundreds mock another day
Because we have made our art of common things,
So bitterly, you'd dream they longed to look
All their lives through into some drift of wings.
You've dandled them and fed them from the book
And know them to the bone; impart us –

We'll keep the secret – a new trick to please.
Is there a bridle for this Proteus
That turns and changes like his draughty seas?
Or is there none, most popular of men,
But when they mock us, that we mock again?

FROM THE GREEK OF SOPHOCLES

I

Colonus' Praise

(*Oedipus at Colonus*, lines 668–719)

CHORUS: Come praise Colonus' horses, and come praise
The wine-dark of the wood's intricacies,
The nightingale that deafens daylight there,
If daylight ever visit where,
Unvisited by tempest or by sun,
Immortal ladies tread the ground
Dizzy with harmonious sound,
Semele's lad a gay companion.

And yonder in the gymnasts' garden thrives
The self-sown, self-begotten shape that gives
Athenian intellect its mastery,
Even the grey-leaved olive-tree
Miracle-bred out of the living stone;
Nor accident of peace nor war
Shall wither that old marvel, for
The great grey-eyed Athena stares thereon.

Who comes into this country, and has come
Where golden crocus and narcissus bloom,
Where the Great Mother, mourning for her daughter
And beauty-drunken by the water
Glittering among grey-leaved olive-trees,
Has plucked a flower and sung her loss;
Who finds abounding Cephisus
Has found the loveliest spectacle there is.

Because this country has a pious mind
And so remembers that when all mankind
But trod the road, or splashed about the shore,
Poseidon gave it bit and oar,
Every Colonus lad or lass discourses
Of that oar and of that bit;
Summer and winter, day and night,
Of horses and horses of the sea, white horses.

2

Chorus from Antigone

(lines 781–805)

Overcome – O bitter sweetness,
Inhabitant of the soft cheek of a girl –
The rich man and his affairs,
The fat flocks and the fields' fatness,
Mariners, rough harvesters;
Overcome Gods upon Parnassus;

Overcome the Empyrean; hurl
Heaven and Earth out of their places,
That in the same calamity
Brother and brother, friend and friend,
Family and family,
City and city may contend,
By that great glory driven wild.

Pray I will and sing I must,
And yet I weep – Oedipus' child
Descends into the loveless dust.

GILBERT MURRAY
(1866–1957)

FROM THE GREEK OF EURIPIDES

I

Dance of the Maidens of Dionysus

From *The Bacchae*

CHORUS

Some Maidens

Will they ever come to me, ever again,
    The long long dances,
On through the dark till the dim stars wane?
Shall I feel the dew on my throat, and the stream
Of wind in my hair? Shall our white feet gleam
    In the dim expanses?
Oh, feet of a fawn to the greenwood fled,
   Alone in the grass and the loveliness;
Leap to the hunted, no more in dread,
   Beyond the snares and the deadly press:
Yet a voice still in the distance sounds,
A voice and a fear and a haste of hounds;
O wildly labouring, fiercely fleet,
    Onward yet by river and glen . . .
Is it joy or terror, ye storm-swift feet? . . .
    To the dear lone lands untroubled of men,
Where no voice sounds, and amid the shadowy green
The little things of the woodland live unseen.

What else is Wisdom? What of man's endeavour
   Or God's high grace, so lovely and so great?
   To stand from fear set free, to breathe and wait;
   To hold a hand uplifted over Hate;
And shall not Loveliness be loved for ever?

FROM THE GREEK OF SOPHOCLES

2

Hymn to Eros

From *Antigone*

CHORUS   [*Strophe*

Erôs, invincible in fight,
   Who ragest in the flocks, Erôs,
   Who hauntest, tender in repose,
A maiden's cheek at night;
Past the deep sea thy pinion flies,
Past where the hidden forest lies;
And none of gods immortal may
Escape thee; how shall humans, they
Whose breath endureth scarce a day?
     The Madman grasps his prize.

                       [*Antistrophe*

Though man be just, by thee his mood
Is warped to wrong and wrecked his life;
'Tis thou, even here, hast wakened strife
   'Tween kinsmen of one blood.
All-conquering is thy spell soft-eyed
That yearneth from the waiting bride;
Beside the eternal laws thy will
Is throned, where, irresistible
And deathless, Aphrodite still
     Mocketh her prisoners' pride.

LEADER

I too beyond the laws am borne,
   And can no more. Who would not weep
To see this maiden, how forlorn
   She moves before us to the deep
   Bride-chamber of eternal sleep?

[*Enter* ANTIGONE *guarded*

ANTIGONE   [*Strophe* 1

Behold, O Land of Thebes, O ye
    My countrymen; I go my last
Journey; and never more shall see
    The sunlight. All is past.
Hades, the Sleep-compeller, goes before
To guide me, living, to the lifeless shore;
No chant of trooping comrades leads me here,
No music for a human bridegroom's ear;
The bride of Acheron I for evermore.

CHORUS

Therefore in glory and high praise
To yon dead vault thou goest thy ways;
No wasting sickness shalt thou fear,
No wages of the sword are here.
Alone and mistress of thy fate
Thou walkest living to the gate
Of Death, from all men separate.

ANTIGONE   [*Antistrophe* 1

I have heard how perished piteous
    That Phrygian stranger, once our own,
'Gainst a high crag on Sipylus.
    As ivy climbs, the stone
Climbed and subdued her, and there wasteth she –
So still abides the ancient history –
And the rains never leave her, nor the snow,
And the dim crown weeps on the breast below;
To stone go I, most like to Niobe.

CHORUS

A goddess she and child of Heaven;
We born to die, of mortal blood;
Is it not grace surpassing, given
To one like thee, of human breath,

To have shared the suffering of a god,
    In life, in death?

ANTIGONE   [*Strophe 2*

    Ah, do ye mock me? Nay,
By your forefathers' gods and mine I pray,
Will ye not wait till I have gone my way,
    Not taunt me to my face?
  O banks of Dirce, holy place
  Of Thêbê crowned and charioted;
O mine own City, men of my City, ye
Who are so rich; be witnesses for me,
How poor I go, how all uncomforted
  Of friends, by how unjust a doom,
To this rock prison that shall be my tomb,
From night and day alike disherited,
Homeless on earth, homeless among the dead.

CHORUS

  My daughter, to the extreme height
    Of daring thou hast climbed, and prone
  Flung thee before the Altar-stone
    Of Justice. – Ah, must thou requite
      Wrongs by thy fathers done?

ANTIGONE   [*Antistrophe 2*

    That stirs my bitterest thought,
My thrice-told aching sorrow for the lot
Of mine own father and all the travail-fraught
    Line of our ancient kings.
    Alas, always the memory clings
  Of evil to my mother's bed,
Of ignorance sent from heaven, and infamy
Wrought on her own son – and my father he . . .
How can my thought endure it? . . . Am I not bred
And born from them? Away to them I go,
Childless, accurst, to share their homes below.

O brother, not unloved but most ill-wed,
Thou hast slain me, thou has reached me from the dead.

CHORUS

For man to be not merciless
Is a great part of godliness;
But never Power – so speaks the throne
Which guardeth power – may be defied.
'Tis for the passion of thine own
Resolve thou wilt have died.

ANTIGONE

Alone, alone,
Unwept, unfriended, with no escort song,
They lead me. All is ready for the long
    Road that is all my own.
Ah, never more this holy Sun shall spread
    His light before mine eyes,
Unhappy! Yet for me no tears are shed,
        No comrade sighs.

ERNEST CHRISTOPHER DOWSON
(1867–1900)

FROM THE FRENCH OF PAUL VERLAINE

'Le ciel est, par-dessus le toit'

The sky is up above the roof
    So blue, so soft!
A tree there, up above the roof,
    Swayeth aloft.

A bell within that sky we see,
    Chimes low and faint:
A bird upon that tree we see,
    Maketh complaint.

Dear God! is not the life up there,
    Simple and sweet?
How peacefully are borne up there
    Sounds of the street!

What hast thou done, who comest here,
    To weep alway?
Where hast thou laid, who comest here,
    Thy youth away?

LAURENCE BINYON
(1869–1942)

FROM THE ITALIAN OF DANTE

The Inferno

(Canto XXXIII, lines 38–78)

THE HUNGER OF UGOLINO

'When I awoke dark on my stony bed
   I heard my children weeping in their sleep,
   Them who were with me, and they cried for bread.
Cruel art thou if thou from tears canst keep
   To think of what my heart misgave in fear.
   If thou weep not, at what then canst thou weep?
By now they were awake, and the hour drew near
   When food should be set by us on the floor.
   Still in the trouble of our dreams we were:
And down in the horrible tower I heard the door
   Locked up. Without a word I looked anew.
   Into my sons' faces, all the four.
I wept not, so to stone within I grew.
   They wept; and one, my little Anselm, cried:
   "You look so, Father, what has come to you?"
But I shed not a tear, neither replied
   All that day nor the next night, until dawn
   Of a new day over the world rose wide.
A cranny of light crept in upon the stone
   Of that dungeon of woe; and I saw there
   On those four faces the aspect of my own.
I bit upon both hands in my despair.
   And they supposing it was in the access
   Of hunger, rose up with a sudden prayer,
And said: "O Father, it will hurt much less
   If you of us eat: take what once you gave
   To clothe us, this flesh of our wretchedness."
Thereon I calmed myself, their grief to save.
   That day and the one after we were dumb.

Hard earth, couldst thou not open for our grave?
But when to the fourth morning we were come,
   Gaddo at my feet stretched himself with a cry:
   "Father, why won't you help me?" and lay numb
And there died. Ev'n as thou seest me, saw I,
   One after the other, the three fall. They drew,
   Between the fifth and sixth day, their last sigh.
I, blind now, groping arms about them threw,
   And still called on them that were two days dead.
   Then fasting did what anguish could not do.'
He ceased, and with eyes twisted in his head
   His teeth seized on the lamentable skull
   Strong as a dog's upon a bony shred.

EDWARD MARSH
(1872–1953)

FROM THE LATIN OF HORACE

Albi ne doleas

(*Odes*, Book 1, 33)

Tibullus, pull yourself together!
You mustn't make such heavy weather
   When women throw you over.
All day you melt in songs of woe,
Merely because a younger beau
   Is now Neaera's lover.

The slender-brow'd Lycoris burns
For Cyrus: presto, Cyrus turns
   To court the peevish Julia;
But Julia will no more abate
Her virgin pride, than does will mate
   With wolves from wild Apulia.

Thus Venus plays her grimmest joke;
She loves to match beneath her yoke
   Those who have least in common,
And both in looks and characters
Concocts the most unlikely pairs –
   No help for man or woman!

Take my own case: I might have wooed
A girl as fair as she was good,
   And here you see me slaving,
In utter bliss, for Myrtale,
A slut, more tetchy than the sea
   Round southern headlands raving.

MAURICE BARING
(1874–1945)

I

Remembrance

When the loud day for men who sow and reap
Grows still, and on the silence of the town
The unsubstantial veils of night and sleep,
The meed of the day's labour, settle down,
Then for me in the stillness of the night
The wasting, watchful hours drag on their course,
And in the idle darkness comes the bite
Of all the burning serpents of remorse;
Dreams seethe; and fretful infelicities
Are swarming in my over-burdened soul,
And Memory before my wakeful eyes
With noiseless hand unwinds her lengthy scroll.
Then, as with loathing I peruse the years,
I tremble, and I curse my natal day,
Wail bitterly, and bitterly shed tears,
But cannot wash the woeful script away.

2

The Prophet

With fainting soul athirst for Grace,
I wandered in a desert place,
And at the crossing of the ways
I saw a sixfold Seraph blaze;
He touched mine eyes with fingers light
As sleep that cometh in the night:
And like a frighted eagle's eyes,
They opened wide with prophecies.

He touched mine ears, and they were drowned
With tumult and a roaring sound:
I heard convulsion in the sky,
And flight of angel hosts on high,
And beasts that move beneath the sea,
And the sap creeping in the tree.
And bending to my mouth he wrung
From out of it my sinful tongue,
And all its lies and idle rust,
And 'twixt my lips a-perishing
A subtle serpent's forkèd sting
With right hand wet with blood he thrust.
And with his sword my breast he cleft,
My quaking heart thereout he reft,
And in the yawning of my breast
A coal of living fire he pressed.
Then in the desert I lay dead,
And God called unto me and said:
'Arise, and let My voice be heard,
Charged with My will go forth and span
The land and sea, and let My word
Lay waste with fire the heart of man.'

GILBERT KEITH CHESTERTON
(1874–1936)

FROM THE FRENCH OF JOACHIM DU BELLAY

'*Happy, who like Ulysses . . .*'

Happy, who like Ulysses or that lord
   Who raped the fleece, returning full and sage,
With usage and the world's wide reason stored,
   With his own kin can wait the end of age.
When shall I see, when shall I see, God knows!
   My little village smoke; or pass the door,
The old dear door of that unhappy house
   That is to me a kingdom and much more?
Mightier to me the house my fathers made
   Than your audacious heads, O Halls of Rome!
More than immortal marbles undecayed,
   The thin sad slates that cover up my home;
More than your Tiber is my Loire to me,
   Than Palatine my little Lyré there;
And more than all the winds of all the sea
   The quiet kindness of the Angevin air.

ADRIAAN BARNOUW
(b. 1877)

FROM THE DUTCH OF PETRUS AUGUSTUS DE GENESTET

Such is Holland!

O, land of mud and mist, where man is wet and shivers
    Soaked with humidity, with damp and chilly dew,
    O, land of unplumbed bogs, of roads resembling rivers,
Land of umbrellas, gout, colds, agues, toothache, flu,

O, spongy porridge-swamp, O homeland of galoshes,
    Of cobblers, toads, and frogs, peat diggers, mildew, mould,
Of ducks and every bird that slobbers, splutters, splashes,
    Hear the autumnal plaint of a poet with a cold.

Thanks to your clammy clime my arteries are clotted
    With blood turned mud. No song, no joy, no peace for me.
    You're fit for clogs alone, O land our forebears plotted
And, not at my request, extorted from the sea.

JOHN MASEFIELD
(b. 1878)

Sonnet

I saw the ramparts of my native land,
One time so strong, now dropping in decay,
Their strength destroyed by this new age's way,
That has worn out and rotted what was grand.

I went into the fields: there I could see
The sun drink up the waters newly thawed,
And on the hills the moaning cattle pawed;
Their miseries robbed the day of light for me.

I went into my house: I saw how spotted,
Decaying things made that old home their prize.
My withered walking-staff had come to bend.
I felt the age had won; my sword was rotted,
And there was nothing on which to set my eyes
That was not a reminder of the end.

JAMES JOYCE
(1882–1941)

FROM THE GERMAN OF GOTTFRIED KELLER

'Now have I fed and eaten up the rose'

Now have I fed and eaten up the rose
Which then she laid within my stiffcold hand.
That I should ever feed upon a rose
I never had believed in liveman's land.

Only I wonder was it white or red
The flower that in the dark my food has been.
Give us, and if Thou give, thy daily bread,
Deliver us from evil, Lord, Amen.

EZRA POUND
(b. 1885)

FROM THE ITALIAN OF GUIDO CAVALCANTI

Sonnet XXX

I fear me lest unfortune's counter thrust
Pierce through my throat and rip out my despair.
I feel my heart and that thought shaking there
Which shakes the aspen mind with his distrust,

Seeming to say, 'Love doth not give thee ease
So that thou canst, as of a little thing,
Speak to thy Lady with full verities,
For fear Death set thee in his reckoning.

By the chagrin that here assails my soul
My heart's parturèd of a sigh so great
It cryeth to the spirits: 'Get ye gone!'

And of all piteous folk I come on none
Who seeing me so in my grief's control
Will aid by saying e'en: 'Nay, Spirits, wait!'

FROM THE LATIN OF ANDREA NAVAGERO

Inscriptio Fontis

Lo! the fountain is cool and
 none more hale of waters.
Green is the land about it,
 soft with the grasses.
And twigged boughs of elm
 stave off the sun.

There is no place more charmed
 with light-blown airs,
Though Titan in utmost flame
 holdeth the middle sky,

And the parched fields burn with
    the oppressing star.

Stay here thy way, O voyager,
    for terrible is now the heat;
Thy tired feet can go no further now.
Balm here for weariness is
    sweet reclining,
Balm 'gainst the heat, the winds,
    and greeny shade!
And for thy thirst the lucid fount's assuaging.

FROM THE ANGLO-SAXON

The Seafarer

May I for my own self song's truth reckon,
Journey's jargon, how I in harsh days
Hardship endured oft.
Bitter breast-cares have I abided,
Known on my keel many a care's hold,
And dire sea-surge, and there I oft spent
Narrow nightwatch nigh the ship's head
While she tossed close to cliffs. Coldly afflicted,
My feet were by frost benumbed.
Chill its chains are; chafing sighs
Hew my heart round and hunger begot
Mere-weary mood. Lest man know not
That he on dry land loveliest liveth,
List how I, care-wretched, on ice-cold sea,
Weathered the winter, wretched outcast
Deprived of my kinsmen;
Hung with hard ice-flakes, where hail-scur flew,
There I heard naught save the harsh sea
And ice-cold wave, at whiles the swan cries,
Did for my games the gannet's clamour,
Sea-fowls' loudness was for me laughter,
The mews' singing all my mead-drink.
Storms, on the stone-cliffs beaten, fell on the stern

In icy feathers; full oft the eagle screamed
With spray on his pinion.

                              Not any protector
May make merry man faring needy.
This he little believes, who aye in winsome life
Abides 'mid burghers some heavy business,
Wealthy and wine-flushed, how I weary oft
Must bide above brine.
Neareth nightshade, snoweth from north,
Frost froze the land, hail fell on earth then,
Corn of the coldest. Nathless there knocketh now
The heart's thought that I on high streams
The salt-wavy tumult traverse alone.
Moaneth alway my mind's lust
That I fare forth, that I afar hence
Seek out a foreign fastness.
For this there's no mood-lofty man over earth's midst,
Not though he be given his good, but will have in his youth greed;
Nor his deed to the daring, nor his king to the faithful
But shall have his sorrow for sea-fare
Whatever his lord will.
He hath not heart for harping, nor in ring-having
Nor winsomeness to wife, nor world's delight
Nor any whit else save the wave's slash,
Yet longing comes upon him to fare forth on the water.
Bosque taketh blossom, cometh beauty of berries,
Fields to fairness, land fares brisker,
All this admonisheth man eager of mood,
The heart turns to travel so that he then thinks
On flood-ways to be far departing.
Cuckoo calleth with gloomy crying,
He singeth summerward, bodeth sorrow,
The bitter heart's blood. Burgher knows not –
He the prosperous man – what some perform
Where wandering them widest draweth.
So that but now my heart burst from my breastlock,
My mood 'mid the mere-flood,
Over the whale's acre, would wander wide.
On earth's shelter cometh oft to me,

Eager and ready, the crying lone-flyer,
Whets for the whale-path the heart irresistibly,
O'er tracks of ocean; seeing that anyhow
My lord deems to me this dead life
On loan and on land, I believe not
That any earth-weal eternal standeth
Save there be somewhat calamitous
That, ere a man's tide go, turn it to twain.
Disease or oldness or sword-hate
Beats out the breath from doom-gripped body.
And for this, every earl whatever, for those speaking after —
Laud of the living, boasteth some last word,
That he will work ere he pass onward,
Frame on the fair earth 'gainst foes his malice,
Daring ado, . . .
So that all men shall honour him after
And his laud beyond them remain 'mid the English,
Aye, for ever, a lasting life's-blast,
Delight 'mid the doughty.
                        Days little durable,
And all arrogance of earthen riches,
There come now no kings nor Caesars
Nor gold-giving lords like those gone.
Howe'er in mirth most magnified,
Whoe'er lived in life most lordliest,
Drear all this excellence, delights undurable!
Waneth the watch, but the world holdeth.
Tomb hideth trouble. The blade is layed low.
Earthly glory ageth and seareth.
No man at all going the earth's gait,
But age fares against him, his face paleth,
Grey-haired he groaneth, knows gone companions,
Lordly men, are to earth o'ergiven,
Nor may he then the flesh-cover, whose life ceaseth,
Nor eat the sweet nor feel the sorry,
Nor stir hand nor think in mid heart,
And though he strew the grave with gold,
His born brothers, their buried bodies
Be an unlikely treasure hoard.

FROM THE ENGLISH VERSIONS OF THE HINDI
BY KALI MOHAN GHOSE

A Poem of Kabir

It is true, I am mad with love. And what to me
Is carefulness or uncarefulness?
Who, dying, wandering in the wilderness,
Who is separated from the dearest?
My dearest is within me, what do I care?
The beloved is not asundered from me,
No, not for the veriest moment.
And I also am not asundered from him.
My love clings to him only.
Where is restlessness in me?
Oh my mind dances with joy,
Dances like a mad fool.
The rāginis of love are being played day and night,
All are listening to that measure.
Rāhu, the eclipse, Ketu, the Head of the Dragon,
And the nine planets are dancing,
And Birth and Death are dancing, mad with Ananda.
The mountain, the sea and the earth are dancing,
The Great Adornment is dancing with laughter and tears and
    smiles.
Why are you leaving 'the world',
You, with the *tilak*-mark on your forehead?
While my mind is a-dancing through the thousand stages of its
    moon,
And the Lord of all his creation has found it acceptable dancing.

CATHAY

FROM THE CHINESE OF BUNNO

Song of the Bowmen of Shu

Here we are, picking the first fern-shoots
And saying: When shall we get back to our country?

Here we are because we have the Ken-nin for our foemen,
We have no comfort because of these Mongols.
We grub the soft fern-shoots,
When anyone says 'Return', the others are full of sorrow.
Sorrowful minds, sorrow is strong, we are hungry and thirsty.
Our defence is not yet made sure, no one can let his friend return.
We grub the old fern-stalks.
We say: Will we be let to go back in October?
There is no ease in royal affairs, we have no comfort.
Our sorrow is bitter, but we would not return to our country.
What flower has come into blossom?
Whose chariot? The General's.
Horses, his horses even, are tired. They were strong.
We have no rest, three battles a month.
By heaven, his horses are tired.
The generals are on them, the soldiers are by them.
The horses are well trained, the generals have ivory arrows and
    quivers ornamented with fish-skin.
The enemy is swift, we must be careful.
When we set out, the willows were drooping with spring,
We come back in the snow,
We go slowly, we are hungry and thirsty,
Our mind is full of sorrow, who will know of our grief?

FROM THE CHINESE OF MEI SHENG

The Beautiful Toilet

Blue, blue is the grass about the river
And the willows have overfilled the close garden.
And within, the mistress, in the midmost of her youth,
White, white of face, hesitates, passing the door.
Slender, she put forth a slender hand;

And she was a courtezan in the old days,
And she has married a sot,
Who now goes drunkenly out
And leaves her too much alone.

FROM THE CHINESE OF RIHAKU

I

The River Song

This boat is of shato-wood, and its gunwales are cut magnolia,
Musicians with jewelled flutes and with pipes of gold
Fill full the sides in rows, and our wine
Is rich for a thousand cups.
We carry singing girls, drift with the drifting water,
Yet Sennin needs
A yellow stork for a charger, and all our seamen
Would follow the white gulls or ride them.
Kutsu's prose song
Hangs with the sun and moon.
King So's terraced palace
                        is now but barren hill,
But I draw pen on this barge
Causing the five peaks to tremble,
And I have joy in these words
                        like the joy of blue islands.
(If glory could last forever
Then the waters of Han would flow northward.)
And I have moped in the Emperor's garden, awaiting an order-to-
    write!
I looked at the dragon-pond, with its willow-coloured water
Just reflecting the sky's tinge,
And heard the five-score nightingales aimlessly singing.

The eastern wind brings the green colour into the island grasses at
    Yei-shu,
The purple house and the crimson are full of Spring softness.
South of the pond the willow-tips are half-blue and bluer,
Their cords tangle in mist, against the brocade-like palace.
Vine-strings a hundred feet long hang down from carved railings,
And high over the willows, the fine birds sing to each other, and
    listen,
Crying – 'Kwan, Kuan', for the early wind, and the feel of it.
The wind bundles itself into a bluish cloud and wanders off.

Over a thousand gates, over a thousand doors are the sounds of
    spring singing,
And the Emperor is at Ko.
Five clouds hang aloft, bright on the purple sky,
The imperial guards come forth from the golden house with their
  armour a-gleaming.
The Emperor in his jewelled car goes out to inspect his flowers,
He goes out to Hori, to look at the wing-flapping storks,
He returns by way of Sei rock, to hear the new nightingales,
For the gardens at Jo-run are full of new nightingales,
Their sound is mixed in this flute,
Their voice is in the twelve pipes here.

2

The River Merchant's Wife: A Letter

While my hair was still cut straight across my forehead
I played about the front gate, pulling flowers.
You came by on bamboo stilts, playing horse,
You walked about my seat, playing with blue plums.
And we went on living in the village of Chokan:
Two small people, without dislike or suspicion.

At fourteen I married My Lord you.
I never laughed, being bashful.
Lowering my head, I looked at the wall.
Called to, a thousand times, I never looked back.

At fifteen I stopped scowling,
I desired my dust to be mingled with yours
Forever and forever and forever.
Why should I climb the look out?

At sixteen you departed.
You went into far Ku-to-yen, by the river of swirling eddies,
And you have been gone five months.
The monkeys make sorrowful noise overhead.

You dragged your feet when you went out.
By the gate now, the moss is grown, the different mosses,

Too deep to clear them away!
The leaves fall early this autumn, in wind.
The paired butterflies are already yellow with August
Over the grass in the West garden;
They hurt me. I grow older.
If you are coming down through the narrows of the river Kiang,
Please let me know beforehand,
And I will come out to meet you
                    As far as Cho-fu-Sa.

3

The Jewel Stairs' Grievance

The jewelled steps are already quite white with dew,
It is so late that the dew soaks my gauze stockings,
And I let down the crystal curtain
And watch the moon through the clear autumn.

4

Lament of the Frontier Guard

By the North Gate, the wind blows full of sand,
Lonely from the beginning of time until now!
Trees fall, the grass goes yellow with autumn.
I climb the towers and towers
        to watch out the barbarous land:
Desolate castle, the sky, the wide desert.
There is no wall left to this village.
Bones white with a thousand frosts,
High heaps, covered with trees and grass;
Who brought this to pass?
Who has brought the flaming imperial anger?
Who has brought the army with drums and with kettle-drums?
Barbarous kings.
A gracious spring, turned to blood-ravenous autumn,
A turmoil of wars-men, spread over the middle kingdom,
Three hundred and sixty thousand,

And sorrow, sorrow like rain.
Sorrow to go, and sorrow, sorrow returning.
Desolate, desolate fields,
And no children of warfare upon them,
      No longer the men for offence and defence.
Ah, how shall you know the dreary sorrow at the
      North Gate,
With Rihaku's name forgotten,
And we guardsmen fed to the tigers.

5

Taking Leave of a Friend

Blue mountains to the north of the walls,
White river winding about them;
Here we must make separation
And go out through a thousand miles of dead grass.
Mind like a floating wide cloud,
Sunset like the parting of old acquaintances
Who bow over their clasped hands at a distance.
Our horses neigh to each other
      as we are departing.

FROM THE CHINESE OF T'AO YUAN MING

To-Em-Mei's 'The Unmoving Cloud'

         'Wet springtime,' says To-em-mei,
             'Wet spring in the garden.'

I

The clouds have gathered, and gathered,
      and the rain falls and falls,
The eight ply of the heavens
      are all folded into one darkness,
And the wide, flat road stretches out.
I stop in my room toward the East, quiet, quiet,

I pat my new cask of wine.
My friends are estranged, or far distant,
I bow my head and stand still.

II

Rain, rain, and the clouds have gathered,
The eight ply of the heavens are darkness,
The flat land is turned into river.
       'Wine, wine, here is wine!'
I drink by my eastern window.
I think of talking and man,
And no boat, no carriage, approaches.

III

The trees in my east-looking garden
       are bursting out with new twigs,
They try to stir new affection,
And men say the sun and moon keep on moving
       because they can't find a soft seat.
The birds flutter to rest in my tree,
       and I think I have heard them saying,
'It is not that there are no other men
But we like this fellow the best,
But however we long to speak
He can not know of our sorrow.'

FROM THE GERMAN OF HEINRICH HEINE

I dreamt that I was God Himself
Whom heavenly joy immerses,
And all the angels sat about
And praised my verses.

FROM THE LATIN ODYSSEY OF ANDREAS DIVUS

From Canto I

And then went down to the ship,
Set keel to breakers, forth on the godly sea, and
We set up mast and sail on that swart ship,
Bore sheep aboard her, and our bodies also
Heavy with weeping, so winds from sternward
Bore us out onward with bellying canvas,
Circe's this craft, the trim-coifed goddess.
Then sat we amidships, wind jamming the tiller,
Thus with stretched sail, we went over sea till day's end.
Sun to his slumber, shadows o'er all the ocean,
Came we then to the bounds of deepest water,
To the Kimmerian lands, and peopled cities
Covered with close-webbed mist, unpiercèd ever
With glitter of sun-rays
Nor with stars stretched, nor looking back from heaven
Swartest night stretched over wretched men there.
The ocean flowing backward, came we then to the place
Aforesaid by Circe.
Here did they rites, Perimedes and Eurylochus,
And drawing sword from my hip
I dug the ell-square pitkin;
Poured we libations unto each the dead,
First mead and then sweet wine, water mixed with white flour.
Then prayed I many a prayer to the sickly death's-heads;
As set in Ithaca, sterile bulls of the best
For sacrifice, heaping the pyre with goods,
A sheep to Tiresias only, black and a bell-sheep.
Dark blood flowed in the fosse,
Souls out of Erebus, cadaverous dead, of brides,
Of youths and of the old who had borne much;
Souls stained with recent tears, girls tender,
Men many, mauled with bronze lance heads,
Battle spoil, bearing yet dreory arms,
These many crowded about me; with shouting,
Pallor upon me, cried to my men for more beasts;

Slaughtered the herds, sheep slain of bronze;
Poured ointment, cried to the gods,
To Pluto the strong, and praised Proserpine;
Unsheathed the narrow sword,
I sat to keep off the impetuous impotent dead,
Till I should hear Tiresias.
But first Elpenor came, our friend Elpenor,
Unburied, cast on the wide earth,
Limbs that we left in the house of Circe,
Unwept, unwrapped in sepulchre, since toils urged other.
Pitiful spirit. And I cried in hurried speech:
'Elpenor, how art thou come to this dark coast?
'Cam'st thou afoot, outstripping seamen?'
      And he in heavy speech:
'Ill fate and abundant wine. I slept in Circe's ingle.
'Going down the long ladder unguarded,
'I fell against the buttress,
'Shattered the nape-nerve, the soul sought Avernus.
'But thou, O King, I bid remember me, unwept, unburied,
'Heap up mine arms, be tomb by sea-bord, and inscribed:
'*A man of no fortune, and with a name to come.*
'And set my oar up, that I swung mid fellows.'

And Anticlea came, whom I beat off, and then Tiresias Theban,
Holding his golden wand, knew me, and spoke first:
'A second time? why? man of ill star,
'Facing the sunless dead and this joyless region?
'Stand from the fosse, leave me my bloody bever
'For soothsay.'
      And I stepped back,
And he strong with the blood, said then: 'Odysseus
'Shalt return through spiteful Neptune, over dark seas,
'Lose all companions.' Then Anticlea came.
Lie quiet Divus. I mean, that is Andreas Divus,
In officina Wecheli, 1538, out of Homer.

FROM THE LATIN

Homage to Sextus Propertius

III

Midnight, and a letter comes to me from our mistress:
           Telling me to come to Tibur, *At* once!!
Bright tips reach up from twin towers,
           Anenian spring water falls into flat-spread pools.

What *is* to be done about it?
           Shall I entrust myself to entangled shadows,
Where bold hands may do violence to my person?

Yet if I postpone my obedience
                  because of this respectable terror
I shall be prey to lamentations worse than a nocturnal assailant.
And I shall be in the wrong,
               and it will last a twelve month,
For her hands have no kindness me-ward,

Nor is there anyone to whom lovers are not sacred at midnight
And in the Via Sciro.

If any man would be a lover
               he may walk on the Scythian coast,
No barbarism would go to the extent of doing him harm,
The moon will carry his candle,
             the stars will point out the stumbles,
Cupid will carry lighted torches before him
             and keep mad dogs off his ankles.
Thus all roads are perfectly safe
            and at any hour;
Who so indecorous as to shed the pure gore of a suitor?!
        Cypris is his cicerone.
What if undertakers follow my track,
             such a death is worth dying.
She would bring frankincense and wreaths to my tomb,
           She would sit like an ornament on my pyre.

Gods' aid, let not my bones lie in a public location
     with crowds too assiduous in their crossing of it;
For thus are tombs of lovers most desecrated.

May a woody and sequestered place cover me with its foliage
Or may I inter beneath the hummock
      of some as yet uncatalogued sand;
At any rate I shall not have my epitaph in a high road.

VI

When, when, and whenever death closes our eyelids,
Moving naked over Acheron
    Upon the one raft, victor and conquered together,
Marius and Jugurtha together,
       one tangle of shadows.
Caesar plots against India,
Tigris and Euphrates shall, from now on, flow at his bidding,
Tibet shall be full of Roman policemen,
The Parthians shall get used to our statuary
       and acquire a Roman religion;

One raft on the veiled flood of Acheron,
    Marius and Jugurtha together.
Nor at my funeral either will there be any long trail,
      bearing ancestral lares and images;
No trumpets filled with my emptiness,
Nor shall it be on an Atalic bed;
    The perfumed cloths shall be absent.
A small plebeian procession.
    Enough, enough and in plenty
There will be three books at my obsequies
Which I take, my not unworthy gift, to Persephone.

You will follow the bare scarified breast
Nor will you be weary of calling my name, nor too weary
    To place the last kiss on my lips
When the Syrian onyx is broken.
    'HE WHO IS NOW VACANT DUST
    'WAS ONCE THE SLAVE OF ONE PASSION':

Give that much inscription
                    'Death why tardily come?'
You, sometimes, will lament a lost friend
            For it is a custom:
This care for past men,

Since Adonis was gored in Idalia, and the Cytherean
Ran crying with out-spread hair,
            In vain, you call back the shade,
In vain, Cynthia. Vain call to unanswering shadow,
            Small talk comes from small bones.

IX

1

The twisted rhombs ceased their clamour of accompaniment.
The scorched laurel lay in the fire-dust,
And the moon still declined wholly to descend out of heaven.

But the black ominous owl hoot was audible,

And one raft bears our fates
                    on the veiled lake toward Avernus
Sails spread on Cerulean waters, I would shed tears for two;
I shall live, if she continue in life.
            If she dies, I shall go with her.
Great Zeus, save the woman,
                    or she will sit before your feet in a veil,
                    and tell out the long list of her troubles.

2

Persephone and Dis, Dis, have mercy upon her,
There are enough women in hell,
                    quite enough beautiful women
Iope, and Tyro, and Pasiphae, and the formal girls of Achaia,
And out of Troad, and from the Campania,
Death has its tooth in the lot,
                    Avernus lusts for the lot of them,
Beauty is not eternal, no man has perennial fortune,
Slow foot, or swift foot, death delays but for a season.

FROM THE FRENCH OF JOACHIM DU BELLAY

Rome

'Troica Roma resurges.' – PROPERTIUS

O thou new comer who seek'st Rome in Rome
And find'st in Rome no thing thou canst call Roman;
Arches worn old and palaces made common,
Rome's name alone within these walls keeps home.

Behold how pride and ruin can befall
One who hath set the whole world 'neath her laws,
All-conquering, now conquered, because
She is Time's prey and Time consumeth all.

Rome that art Rome's one sole last monument,
Rome that alone hast conquered Rome the town,
Tiber alone, transient and seaward bent,
Remains of Rome. O world, thou unconstant mime!
That which stands firm in thee Time batters down,
And that which fleeteth doth outrun swift time.

FROM THE FRENCH OF JULES LAFORGUE

Pierrots

(Scène courte mais typique)

Your eyes! Since I lost their incandescence
Flat calm engulphs my jibs,
The shudder of *Vae soli* gurgles beneath my ribs.

You should have seen me after the affray,
I rushed about in the most agitated way
Crying: My God, my God, what will she say?!

My soul's antennae are prey to such perturbations,
Wounded by your indirectness in these situations
And your bundle of mundane complications.

Your eyes put me up to it.

I thought: Yes, divine, these eyes, but what exists
Behind them? What's there? Her soul's an affair
    for oculists.

And I am sliced with loyal aesthetics.
Hate tremolos and national frenetics.
In brief, violet is the ground tone of my phonetics.

I am not 'that chap there' nor yet 'The Superb'
But my soul, the sort which harsh sounds disturb,
Is, at bottom, distinguished and fresh as a March herb.

FROM THE LATIN OF HORACE

'This monument will outlast. . .'

(*Odes*, Book III, 30)

This monument will outlast metal and I made it
More durable than the king's seat, higher than pyramids.
Gnaw of the wind and rain?
                  Impotent
The flow of the years to break it, however many.
Bits of me, many bits, will dodge all funeral,
O Libitina-Persephone and, after that,
Sprout new praise. As long as
Pontifex and the quiet girl pace the Capitol
I shall be spoken where the wild flood Aufidus
Lashes, and Daunus ruled the parched farmland:
Power from lowliness: 'First brought Aeolic song to
    Italian fashion' –
Wear pride, work's gain! O Muse Melpomene,
    By your will bind the laurel.
                My hair, Delphic laurel.

FROM THE LATIN OF CATULLUS

(LXXXV)

I hate and love. Why? You may ask but
It beats me. I feel it done to me, and ache.

FROM THE CHINESE

Airs from The Book of Odes

I

Pine boat a-shift
on drift of tide,
for flame in the ear, sleep riven,
driven; rift of the heart in dark
no wine will clear,
nor have I will to playe.

Mind that's no mirror to gulp down all's seen,
brothers I have, on whom I dare not lean,
angered to hear a fact, ready to scold.

My heart no turning-stone, mat to be rolled,
right being right, not whim nor matter of count,
true as a tree on mount.

Mob's hate, chance evils many, gone through,
aimed barbs not few;
at bite of the jest in heart
start up as to beat my breast.

O'ersoaring sun, moon-malleable
alternately
lifting a-sky to wane;
sorrow about the heart like an unwashed shirt, I
clutch here at words,
having no force to fly.

2

Green robe, green robe, lined with yellow,
Who shall come to the end of sorrow?
Green silk coat and yellow skirt,
How forget all my heart-hurt?

Green the silk is, you who dyed it;
Antient measure, now divide it?

Nor fine nor coarse cloth keep the wind
from the melancholy mind;
Only antient wisdom is
solace to man's miseries.

3

Pheasant-cock flies on easy wing,
absent lord, to my sorrowing.

As the bright pheasant flies
wind lowers and lifts the tone;
sorrow: my lord gone out,
I am alone.

Look up to the sun and moon
in my thought the long pain,
the road is so long, how
shall he come again.

Ye hundred gentlemen, conscienceless
in your acts, say true:
He neither hates nor covets,
what wrong shall he do?

4

Pick a fern, pick a fern, ferns are high,
'Home,' I'll say: home, the year's gone by,
no house, no roof, these huns on the hoof.
Work, work, work, that's how it runs,
We are here because of these huns.

Pick a fern, pick a fern, soft as they come,
I'll say 'Home.'
Hungry all of us, thirsty here,
no home news for nearly a year.

Pick a fern, pick a fern, if they scratch,
I'll say 'Home,' what's the catch?

I'll say 'Go home,' now October's come.
King wants us to give it all,
no rest, spring, summer, winter, fall,
Sorrow to us, sorrow to you.
We won't get out of here till we're through.

When it's cherry-time with you,
we'll see the captain's car go thru,
four big horses to pull that load.
That's what comes along our road,
What do you call three fights a month,
and won 'em all?

Four car-horses strong and tall
and the boss who can drive 'em all
as we slog along beside his car,
ivory bow-tips and shagreen case
to say nothing of what we face
sloggin' along in the Hien-yün war.

Willows were green when we set out,
it's blowin' an' snowin' as we go
down this road, muddy and slow,
hungry and thirsty and blue as doubt
(no one feels half of what we know).

FROM THE GREEK OF SOPHOCLES

Women of Trachis

I

KHOROS: CELEBRATION OF HERAKLES' RETURN

KHOROS: SAFE the port, rocky the narrows,
Str. 1   Streams warm to a glaze on Oeta's hill,
             Malis' pool and Dian's beach
             Neath her golden-shafted arrows
                  Ye who live here and disdeign
                  All greek towns less than the Pelean,

Ant. 1
(*fifes, flute
& grosse
caisse*)

SOON shall hear the skirl and din
Of flutes' loud cackle shrill return,
Dear to Holy Muses as
Phoebus' lyre ever was.
     From the valours of his wars
Comes now the God, Alkmene's son
Bearing battle booty home.

Str. 2
(*clarinette,
bassoon*)

TWELVE moons passing,
   night long, and day.
Exile, exile
Knowing never, to come? to stay?
Tears, tears, till grief
Hath wrecked her heart away,
Ere mad Mars should end him
   his working day.

Ant. 1
(*cello, low
register*)

TO PORT, to port.
Boat is still now;
The many oars move not.
   By island shrine ere he come to the town
Day long, day long
If the charm of the gown prove not?
'Tis dipped, aye in the unguent
drenched through it, in every fold.
Told, told,
in all as she had been told.

II

DEATH OF HERAKLES

HERAKLES: Listen first, and show what you're made of,
 my stock. My father told me long ago
 that no living man should kill me,
 but that someone from hell would, and
 that brute of a Centaur has done it.
 The dead beast kills the living me.
 and that fits another odd forecast

breathed out at the Selloi's oak –
Those fellows rough it,
    sleep on the ground, up in the hills there.
I heard it and wrote it down
    under my Father's tree.
Time lives, and it's going on now.
I am released from trouble.
I thought it meant life in comfort.
It doesn't. It means that I die.
For amid the dead there is no work in service.
Come at it that way, my boy, what

SPLENDOUR,
          IT ALL COHERES.

FROM THE FRENCH OF ARTHUR RIMBAUD

Cabaret Vert

Wearing out my shoes, 8th day
On the bad roads, I got into Charleroi.
Bread, butter, at the Green Cabaret
And the ham half cold.

Got my legs stretched out
And was looking at the simple tapestries,
Very nice when the gal with the big bubs
And lively eyes,

Not one to be scared of a kiss and more,
Brought the butter and bread with a grin
And the luke-warm ham on a colored plate,

Pink ham, white fat and a sprig
Of garlic, and a great chope of foamy beer
Gilt by the sun in that atmosphere.

FROM THE ITALIAN OF MONTANARI

1

Autunno

Autumn, so many leaves
pass with the wind, I see
the worn-out rain
gather aloft again.

Aimless or vagabond,
a walking sadness, beyond
the deep-cut road:
horses weary of load.

A whirring noise, new night there
empty in monotone:
the Ave Maria
no prayer.

2

L'Ultima Ora

When the will to singing fails
and there be left him no choice
but to rest without singing voice,
forever, unending, arms crossed,

Let it be by the roadside
where the ditch is wide and deep
and the smell of his fields, in sleep
can come to him, and the note of the robin,

And the elms can be there companionable
to him, as evening draws to its close
in the savor of spring time,
melancholy a little, ending together.

FRANCES CORNFORD
(1886–1960)

AND

STEPHEN SPENDER
(b. 1909)

From the Depth of the Abyss

I

The light and warmth
Trampled dispersed
The bread
Stolen from innocents
The thread of milk
Flung to ferocious beasts

Here and there deep pools of blood
Here and there impetuous fires
Sport for those who mean to live
Live live upon their midden-heaps.

II

In a delirious world
Throats in a tumult and devouring bellies
Their bites for us are sun their spittle moon
Our hurts a casket and our stains a pearl
The rotted breast luke-warm
Rotted the legend of the maternal breast
Of pink and verdigris our tongue
The lovely history of our speech spell-bound

III

These melancholics used not to be mad
They were subdued absorbed shut out
By the dense legions
Of efficient monsters

These melancholics had their age of reason
An age of life
They were not present when it all began
At the Creation
They had no faith in it
And from the first were at a loss to make
Life correspond with time

And bed-clothes winter-stained on hearts
Without a body and on nameless hearts
Spread out a covering of chill disgust
Even at summer's height

IV

Always the solitary will be first
Like a worm in a nut
To reappear along the convolutions
Even of the freshest brain
The solitary learns to sidle past
To stop when he is drunk with solitude
The solitary turns his steps all ways
He loiters pulls up short manoeuvres feints

He moves but then at once
Things move and frighten him
The solitary when they call to him
Come little one come little one Come here
Pretends he has not heard

Embedded in fresh meat
Left like a rusted knife
The solitary stops and stays for ever
The smell of carrion stops and stays for ever
The honeycomb of strength is stuffed with filth.

V

I speak from the bottom of the pit
I see to the bottom of the pit
A man hollowed out like a mine
Like a port without ships
Like a hearth with no fire

You poor sacrificed face
You poor face without form
A composite of every pillaged face
You dreamed of spring of kisses of good will
You dreamed of balconies of sails of journeys
And you knew well the rights and obligations
Of beauty beautiful dismembered face

To hide your shame and horror you will need
Hands that are new hands whole in their employment
Hands busy in the present
And brave even in dreams.

VI

I speak now from the bottom of the pit
The bottom of my chasm
Evening is here the shadows flee away
Evening has made me wise and brotherly
His gloomy doors are opened everywhere
I feel no fear I go in everywhere
And more and more I see the human form
Still without features yet
In a dark corner where the wall is down
Are eyes as clear as mine
Have I grown up Have I a little strength.

VII

We are for our two selves the first soft cloud
In the absurd expanse of cruel bliss

The future freshness
And the first night's rest
To open on a face and eyes made pure and new

These no one will be able to ignore.

HILDA DOOLITTLE
(b. 1886)

FROM THE GREEK OF EURIPIDES

Bird of the Air

(*Ion*, lines 154–183)

ION: Bird
of the air,
O, bright legate,
wing back,
back,
I say,
to Parnassus;
off, off the cornice,
that bright peak,
that gold ledge
is no perch for your feet;
O, eagle,
back,

back
where you hold court,
commanding all birds
with your sharp beak;

bird
of the lake,
O, fair,
fairest
of birds
and beloved of king Phoibos,
O, swan
of the white wing,
the red feet,
wing back,
back, I say,

to lake Delos;
O, voice that is tuned
to his harp-note,
O, throat
must I pierce you
with my dart?
be off,
O, my swan
lest your blood drip
red death
on this beautiful pavement;

bird
of the wood,
must you have gold?
these gifts
were not set here
for bird-nests;
bird,
bird
of the woods,
seek your forests
by the isthmus
or near
river Alpheus,
my dart
warns you,
here it is dangerous
for you
and your fledgelings;
O, be off;
my arrow has no choice,
nor I;
I am the god's
and I obey;

but
O, you birds
of lake and forest,
you swan,

you wood-bird
and you legate
of Zeus,
even as I string my bow,
I pray,
be off,
be off,
for I must slay
intruders here
within the precinct;

back to Parnassus
and your nests,
back,
back,
O, God's majestic legate,
back,
back,
O, swan,
my Lord's delight,
back,
back
O, little birds who sing;
for this,
O, this, I would not kill,
your song
that tells to men,
God's will.

NATALIE DUDDINGTON
(b. 1886)

FROM THE RUSSIAN OF ANNA AKHMATOVA

Love Poems

I

'High in the Sky . . .'

'High in the sky there floated a grey cloud
 Like a spread-out squirrel skin.
 He said: 'I am not sorry that your body
 Will melt in March, fragile snow-girl!'

My hands turned cold inside the fluffy muff
 I felt afraid, I was somehow confused.
 How shall I bring you back, oh fleeting weeks
 Of his short-lived and unsubstantial love?

I want no bitterness and no revenge.
 Let me be dead with the last snow-storm.
 I thought of him in New Year fortune-telling,
 Before the month was out I was his love.

2

The Song of the Last Meeting

My breast felt cold and helpless
 But my tread was light as ever.
 I put upon my right hand
 The glove from the left one.

The steps it seemed, were many
 Yet I knew there were only three.
 Among the maples the autumn whisper
 Begged me: 'Die with me!

'I am deceived, you see, by grievous,
Treacherous, evil fate.'
I answered: 'Darling, darling,
I too. I shall die with thee.'

This is the song of the last meeting.
I looked at the still, dark house.
In the bedroom the candles were burning
With a callous yellow light.

3

'Under the dark veil . . .'

Under the dark veil I clasped my hands.
'Why are you so pale today?'
'Because I made him drink his fill
Of the acrid cup of grief.'

How can I forget it? He staggered,
His mouth was twisted with pain,
I ran down not touching the hand-rail,
I ran all the way to the gate.

Breathless, I cried: 'I was joking.
If you go away, I shall die.'
He smiled a strange, calm smile
And said: 'Do not stand in the wind.'

4

'Like one betrothed . . .'

Like one betrothed I get
Each evening a letter.
And late at night sit down to write
An answer to my friend.

Low in the sky there shines a star
Between two trunks of trees.

So calmly promising to me
That what I dream, shall be.

I am staying with white death
On my way to darkness.
Do no evil, gentle one,
To anyone on earth.

HENRY HART
(b. 1886)

FROM THE CHINESE OF YÜAN TI

Confession

Today, in the hall,
I came upon her – mere concubine! –
Who replaced me in my husband's heart.

I fled out of doors,
And met him face to face.

I tried to look composed,
Threw back my sleeve,
Waved my moon-round fan –
And failed.
I hesitated,
Tried to speak,
But the unwilling words
Stuck in my throat, refused to come.
Try as I would to hold back
The pearl-like tears,
They welled from my downcast lids,
And then I knew
That I loved him still,
And that the pain
Which grips my heart today
Would never, never cease.

MARIANNE MOORE
(b. 1887)

FROM THE FRENCH FABLES OF LA FONTAINE

I

The Fox and the Crow

On his airy perch among the branches
    Master Crow was holding cheese in his beak.
Master Fox, whose pose suggested fragrances,
    Said in language which of course I cannot speak,
        'Aha, superb Sir Ebony, well met.
How black! who else boasts your metallic jet!
        If your warbling were unique
        Rest assured, as you are sleek,
One would say that our wood had hatched nightingales.'
    All aglow, Master Crow tried to run a few scales,
        Risking trills and intervals,
Dropping the prize as his huge beak sang false.
The fox pounced on the cheese and remarked, ' My dear sir,
        Learn that every flatterer
    Lives at the flattered listener's cost:
A lesson worth more than the cheese that you lost.'
        The tardy learner, smarting under ridicule,
Swore he'd learned his last lesson as somebody's fool.

2

The Oak and the Reed

        The oak said to the reed, 'You grow
    Too unprotectedly. Nature has been unfair;
A tiny wren alights, and you are bending low;
        If a fitful breath of air
        Should freshen till ripples show,
        You heed her and lower your head;

Whereas my parasol makes welcome shade each day
And like the Caucasus need never sway,
         However it is buffeted.
Your so-called hurricanes are too faint to fear.
Would that you'd been born beneath this towering tent I've made,
         Which could afford you ample shade;
         Your hazards would not be severe:
         I'd shield you when the lightning played;
         But grow you will, time and again,
On the misty fringe of the wind's domain.
I perceive that you are grievously oppressed.'
The rush said, 'Bless you for fearing that I might be distressed;
         It is you alone whom the winds should alarm.
I bend and do not break. You've seemed consistently
         Impervious to harm –
         Erect when blasts rushed to and fro;
As for the end, who can foresee how things will go?'
Relentless wind was on them instantly –
         A fury of destruction
Which the North had nursed in some haunt known to none.
         The bulrush bent, but not the tree.
         Confusion rose to a roar,
         Until the hurricane threw prone
That thing of kingly height whose head had all but touched God's
                                        throne –
Who had shot his root to the threshold of Death's door.

3

The Fox and the Grapes

A fox of Gascon, though some say of Norman descent,
When starved till faint gazed up at a trellis to which grapes were
                                        tied –
         Matured till they glowed with a purplish tint
         As though there were gems inside.
Now grapes were what our adventurer on strained haunches
                                        chanced to crave,

But because he could not reach the vine
He said, 'These grapes are sour; I'll leave them for some knave.'

Better, I think, than an embittered whine.

4

The Cat and the Rat

Queerer four never were. Cat-claw-the-rind-clean,
Screech-owl-melancholy, Rat-gnaw-the-net,
     Weasel-flatten-out-till-lean –
     Quite an ominous quartet –
Dwelt in a rotting pine, by now only partly green.
Because there were four at the core of the pine,
A man had spread nets, and when the day was fine,
     The cat fared forth to hunt nearby.
Since nets about dawn have ever deceived the eye,
She was forced as their prey, to die it would appear,
Mewing to be set free, until the rat drew near –
She panting in despair and he with hopeful eye
On seeing in a snare his mortal enemy.
     The cat said, 'Blest fortuity!
     Dear guardian, whose plans
     Often helped me in what I sought,
Come aid me tear this net on which I have trod by chance,
     Which snared my foot. Don't leave me caught –
You whom I have held dear and must evermore revere,
Are my favourite, dear to me as my eyes.
I am by no means sad, was offering sacrifice.
     First morning prayers brought me here,
Offered by cats of heartfelt devotion;
The net then bore me down: my life's at your discretion;
Gnaw me free.' The rat inquired, 'Might there be recompense
     To which you have not referred?'
     – 'A pact of mutual defense
     Forever in force,' the cat purred.
'My claws shall be yours; you'll always have the sense

That where I am your enemies dare not stay.
        I shall thin out harmful prey –
        Screech-owl males and weasels in wait,
Thirsting for your blood.' The rat said, 'What a thought,'
        Then hastened homeward obdurate,
        Where he found the weasel a-prowl;
And high on the bole the eyes of the owl.
Selecting the menace which meant him least hurt,
He returned to the cat and plied his art;
Chewed a strand, yet another, on and on
        Till he'd freed the ally he'd hate.
        When the trapper came at dawn
The confederates made off, precipitate,
But as time elapsed it was evident,
As before, that Rat-gnaw was watching every move.
Cat-devour said, 'Embrace me, and seal fair intent;
        My heart is sore, since you prove
        You have thought your friend thinks you her prey.
        Could I forget that yesterday
        With God's help you set me free?'
– 'And I,' replied Rat-gnaw, 'do I know treachery
        Or do I not? Could any say
How one may induce a cat to keep faith two days hence –
        Except by shifts for joint defense
        Favored in an evil day?'

THOMAS STEARNS ELIOT
(1888–1965)

FROM THE FRENCH OF SAINT-JOHN PERSE

Anabasis

I

In busy lands are the greatest silences, in busy lands with the locusts at noon.

I tread, you tread in a land of high slopes clothed in balm, where the linen of the Great is exposed to dry.

We step over the gown of the Queen, all of lace with two brown stripes (and how well the acid body of a woman can stain a gown at the armpit).

We step over the gown of the Queen's daughter, all of lace with two bright stripes (and how well the lizard's tongue can catch ants in the armpit).

And perhaps the day does not pass but the same man may burn with desire for a woman and for her daughter.

Knowing laugh of the dead, let this fruit be peeled for us!... How, under the wild rose is there no more grace to the world?

Comes from this side of the world a great purple doom on the waters. Rises the wind, the sea-wind. And the linen exposed to dry scatters! like a priest torn in pieces. . . .

II

We shall not dwell forever in these yellow lands, our pleasance. . . .

The Summer vaster than the Empire hangs over the tables of space several terraces of climate. The huge earth rolls on its surface over-flowing its pale embers under the ashes – Sulphur colour, honey colour, colour of immortal things, the whole grassy earth taking light from the straw of last winter – and from the green sponge of a lone tree the sky draws its violet juices.

A place glittering with mica! Not a pure grain in the wind's barbs.

And light like oil. – From the crack of my eye to the level of the hills I join myself, I know the stones gillstained, the swarms of silence in the hives of light; and my heart gives heed to a family of locusts. . . .

Like milch-camels, gentle beneath the shears and sewn with mauve scars, let the hills march forth under the scheme of the harvest sky – let them march in silence over the pale incandescence of the plain; and kneel at last, in the smoke of dreams, there where the peoples annihilate themselves in the dead powder of earth.

These are the great quiet lines that disperse in the fading blue of doubtful vines. The earth here and there ripens the violets of storm; and these sandsmokes that rise over dead river courses, like the skirts of centuries on their route. . . .

Lower voice for the dead, lower voice by day. Such gentleness in the heart of man, can it fail to find its measure? . . . 'I speak to you, my soul! – my soul, darkened by the horse smell!' And several great land birds, voyaging westwards, make good likeness of our sea birds.

In the east of so pale a sky, like a holy place sealed by the blind man's linen, calm clouds arrange themselves, where the cancers of camphor and horn revolve. . . . Smoke which a breath of wind claims from us! the earth poised tense in its insect barbs, the earth is brought to bed of wonders! . . .

And at noon, when the jujuba tree breaks the tombstone, man closes his lids and cools his neck in the ages. . . . Horse-tramplings of dreams in the place of dead powders, O vain ways a breath sweeps smoking toward us! where find, where find, the warriors who shall watch the streams in the nuptials?

At the sound of great waters on march over the earth, all the salt of the earth shudders in dream. And sudden, ah sudden, what would these voices with us? Levy a wilderness of mirrors on the boneyard of streams, let them appeal in the course of ages! Raise stones to my fame, raise stones to silence; and to guard these places, cavalcades of green bronze on the great causeways! . . .

(The shadow of a great bird falls on my face.)

RONALD KNOX
(1888–1957)

Lamentations of the Prophet Jeremias:
An alphabet of Patience in Misery

Ah, what straits have I not known, under the avenging rod!
  Asked I for light, into deeper shadow the Lord's guidance led me;
  Always upon me, none other, falls endlessly the blow.
  Broken this frame, under the wrinkled skin, the sunk flesh.
  Bitterness of despair fills my prospect, walled in on every side;
  Buried in darkness, and, like the dead, interminably.
  Closely he fences me in, beyond hope of rescue; loads me with
etters.
  Cry out for mercy as I will, prayer of mine wins no audience;
  Climb these smooth walls I may not; every way of escape he has
undone.
  Deep ambushed he lies, as lurking bear or lion from the covert;
  Drawn aside from my path, I fall a lonely prey to his ravening.
  Dread archer, of me he makes a target for all his arrows;
  Each shaft of his quiver at my vitals taught to strike home!
  Evermore for me the taunts of my neighbours, their songs of
lerision.
  Entertainment of bitter herbs he gives me, and of wormwood my
ill,
  Files all my teeth with hard gravelstones, bids me feed on ashes.
  Far away is my old contentment, happier days forgotten;
  Farewell, my hopes of long continuance, my patient trust in the
Lord!
  Guilt and suffering, gall and wormwood, keep all this well in
memory.
  God knows it shall be remembered, and with sinking of the
heart;
  Gage there can be none other of remaining confidence.
  His be the thanks if we are not extinguished; his mercies never
weary;

127

Hope comes with each dawn; art thou not faithful, Lord, to thy promise?

Heart whispers, The Lord is my portion; I will trust him yet.

In him be thy trust, for him thy heart's longing, gracious thou shalt find him;

If deliverance thou wouldst have from the Lord, in silence await it.

It is well thou shouldst learn to bear the yoke, now in thy youth,

Just burden, in solitude and silence justly borne.

Joy may yet be thine, for mouth that kisses the dust,

Jeering of the multitude, and cheek buffeted in scorn, bravely endured.

Know for certain, the Lord has not finally abandoned thee;

Kind welcome the outcast shall have, from one so rich in kindness.

Kin of Adam he will not crush or cast away wantonly;

Let there be oppression of the poor under duress,

Law's right denied, such as the most High grants to all men,

Lying perversion of justice, then he cannot overlook it.

Man may foretell; only the Lord brings his word to pass;

Mingled good and evil proceed both from the will of the most High;

Mortal is none may repine; let each his own sins remember.

Narrowly our path scan we, and to the Lord return;

Never hand or heart but must point heavenward this day!

Nothing but defiant transgression on our part; and shouldst thou relent?

Over our heads thy angry vengeance lowered; smiting, thou wouldst not spare.

Oh, barrier of cloud, our prayers had no strength to pierce!

Offscouring and refuse of mankind thou hast made us,

Put to shame by the mocking grimaces of our enemies.

Prophets we had, but their word was peril and pitfall, and ruin at the last.

Poor Sion, for thy calamity these cheeks are furrowed with tears;

Quell if thou wouldst the restless fever of my weeping,

Quickly, Lord, look down from heaven and pay heed to us,

Quite forspent, eye and soul, with grief Jerusalem's daughters bear.

Relentless as hawk in air they pursued me, enemies unprovoked,

Reft me of life itself, sealed with a stone my prison door.

Round my head the waters closed, and I had given myself up for lost,

Save for one hope; to thee, Lord, I cried from the pit's depth,

Sure of thy audience; wouldst thou turn a deaf ear to sighs of complaint?

Summoned, thou didst come to my side, whispering, Do not be afraid.

Thine, Lord, to take my part; thine to rescue me from death;

The malice of my enemies to discover, my wrongs to redress.

Thrust away from thy sight, the grudge they bear me, the ill they purpose,

Unheard by thee their taunts, their whispered plottings?

Uttered aloud or in secret, their malice assails me from morn till night;

Up in arms, or met in secret conclave, ever against me they raise the battle-song.

Visit them with the punishment their ill deeds have earned;

Veiled be those blind hearts with fresh blindness of thy own making;

Vanish from the earth their whole brood, ere thy vengeance leaves off pursuing them!

HELEN WADDELL

(1889–1965)

FROM THE MEDIEVAL LATIN OF AUSONIUS

The Fields of Sorrow

They wander in deep woods, in mournful light,
Amid long reeds and drowsy headed poppies,
And lakes where no wave laps, and voiceless streams,
Upon whose banks in the dim light grow old
Flowers that were once bewailèd names of kings.

FROM THE MEDIEVAL LATIN OF BOETHIUS

Cerberus at Hell's gate was still,
    Dazed captive to an unknown song:
No longer plunged the turning wheel,
    And Tantalus, athirst so long,

Heeded the streams no more: the three
    Avenging goddesses of ill
Wept, sad at heart; of melody
    The very vulture drank his fill.

'Yea, thou hast conquered,' said the Lord
    Of Shadows, 'Take her, but be wise.
Thy song hath brought her, but on her
    Turn not, this side of Hell, thine eyes.'

Yet is not Love his greater law?
    And who for lovers shall decree?
On the sheer threshold of the night
    Orpheus saw Eurydice.

Looked, and destroyed her. Ye who read,
    Look up: the gods in daylight dwell.
All that you hold of loveliness
    Sinks from you, looking down at Hell.

FROM THE
MEDIEVAL LATIN OF VENANTIUS FORTUNATUS

Written on an Island off the Breton Coast

You at God's altar stand, His minister,
    And Paris lies about you and the Seine:
Around this Breton isle the Ocean swells,
    Deep water and one love between us twain.

Wild is the wind, but still thy name is spoken;
    Rough is the sea: it sweeps not o'er thy face.
Still runs my love for shelter to its dwelling,
    Hither, O heart, to thine abiding place.

Swift as the waves beneath an east wind breaking
    Dark as beneath a winter sky the sea,
So to my heart crowd memories awaking,
    So dark, O love, my spirit without thee.

FROM THE MEDIEVAL LATIN OF ST COLUMBA

The Day of Wrath

Day of the king most righteous,
    The day is nigh at hand,
The day of wrath and vengeance,
    And darkness on the land.

Day of thick clouds and voices,
    Of mighty thundering,
A day of narrow anguish
    And bitter sorrowing.

The love of women's over,
    And ended is desire,
Men's strife with men is quiet,
    And the world lusts no more.

FROM THE
MEDIEVAL LATIN OF A TENTH-CENTURY MS.

Aubade

Hyperion's clear star is not yet risen,
Dawn brings a tenuous light across the earth,
The watcher to the sleeper cries, 'Arise!'
Dawn over the dark sea brings on the sun;
She leans across the hilltop: see, the light!

Behold the ambush of the enemy
Stealing to take the heedless in their sleep,
And still the herald's voice that cries 'Arise!'
Dawn over the dark sea brings on the sun;
She leans across the hilltop: see, the light!

The North wind from Arcturus now blows free,
The stars go into hiding in the sky,
And nearer to the sunrise swings the Plough.
Dawn over the dark sea brings on the sun;
She leans across the hilltop: see, the light!

ARTHUR WALEY
(1889–1966)

FROM THE CHINESE (ANON.)

The Eastern Castle

The Eastern Castle stands tall and high;
Far and wide stretch the towers that guard it.
The whirling wind uprises and shakes the earth;
The autumn grasses grow thick and green.
The four seasons alternate without pause,
The year's end hurries swiftly on.
The Bird of the Morning Wind is stricken with sorrow;
The frail cicada suffers and is hard pressed.
Free and clear, let us loosen the bonds of our hearts.
Why should we go on always restraining and binding?
In Yen and Chao are many fair ladies,
Beautiful people with faces like jade.
Their clothes are made all of silk gauze,
They stand at the door practising tranquil lays.
The echo of their singing, how sad it sounds!
By the pitch of the song one knows the stops have been tightened.
To ease their minds they arrange their shawls and belts;
Lowering their song, a little while they pause.
'I should like to be those two flying swallows
Who are carrying clay to nest in the eaves of your house.'

FROM THE CHINESE OF PAO CHAO

The Red Hills

Red hills lie athwart us as a menace in the west,
And fiery mountains glare terrible in the south.
The body burns, the head aches and throbs:
If a bird light here, its soul forthwith departs.
Warm springs
Pour from cloudy pools

And hot smoke issues between the rocks.
The sun and moon are perpetually obscured:
The rain and dew never stay dry.
There are red serpents a hundred feet long,
And black snakes ten girths round.
The sand-spitters shoot their poison at the sunbeams:
The flying insects are ill with the shifting glare.
The hungry monkeys dare not come down to eat:
The morning birds dare not set out to fly.
At the Ching river many die of poison:
Crossing the Lu one is lucky if one is only ill.
Our living feet walk on dead ground:
Our high wills surmount the snares of Fate.
The Spear-boat General got but little honour:
The Wave-subduer met with scant reward.
If our Prince still grudges the things that are easy to give,
Can he hope that his soldiers will give what is hardest to give?

FROM THE CHINESE OF SU TUNG-P'O

On the Birth of his Son

Families, when a child is born
Want it to be intelligent.
I, through intelligence,
Having wrecked my whole life,
Only hope the baby will prove
Ignorant and stupid.
Then he will crown a tranquil life
By becoming a Cabinet Minister.

FROM THE CHINESE OF PO CHÜ-I

The Charcoal-Seller

(A Satire against 'Kommandatur')

An old charcoal-seller
Cutting wood and burning charcoal in the forests of the Southern
    Mountain.

His face, stained with dust and ashes, has turned to the colour of
smoke.
The hair on his temples is streaked with grey: his ten fingers are
black.
The money he gets by selling charcoal, how far does it go?
It is just enough to clothe his limbs and put food in his mouth.
Although, alas, the coat on his back is a coat without lining,
He hopes for the coming of cold weather, to send up the price of
coal!
Last night, outside the city, – a whole foot of snow;
At dawn he drives the charcoal wagon along the frozen ruts.
Oxen, – weary; man, – hungry; the sun, already high;
Outside the Gate, to the south of the Market, at last they stop in
the mud.
Suddenly, a pair of prancing horsemen. Who can it be coming?
A public official in a yellow coat and a boy in a white shirt.
In their hands they hold a written warrant: on their tongues – the
words of an order;
They turn back the wagon and curse the oxen, leading them off to
the north.
A whole wagon of charcoal,
More than a thousand catties!
If officials choose to take it away, the woodman may not
complain.
Half a piece of red silk and a single yard of damask,
The Courtiers have tied to the oxen's collar, as the price of a
wagon of coal!

FROM THE CHINESE OF SHU HSI

Hot Cake

Winter has come; fierce is the cold;
In the sharp morning air new-risen we meet.
Rheum freezes in the nose;
Frost hangs about the chin.
For hollow bellies, for chattering teeth and shivering knees
What better than hot cake?

Soft as the down of spring,
Whiter than autumn wool!
Dense and swift the steam
Rises, swells and spreads.
Fragrance flies through the air,
Is scattered far and wide,
Steals down along the wind and wets
The covetous mouth of passer-by.
Servants and grooms
Throw sidelong glances, munch the empty air.
They lick their lips who serve;
While lines of envious lackeys by the wall
Stand dryly swallowing.

FROM THE CHINESE OF CHANG HĒNG

The Dancers of Huai-nan

(A Fragment)

I saw them dancing at Huai-nan and made this poem of praise:

The instruments of music are made ready,
Strong wine is in our cups;
Flute-songs flutter and a din of magic drums.
Sound scatters like foam, surges free as a flood. . . .
And now when the drinkers were all drunken,
And the sun had fallen to the west,
Up rose the fair ones to the dance,
Well painted and apparelled,
In veils of soft gossamer
All wound and meshed;
And ribbons they unravelled,
And scarfs to bind about their heads.
The wielder of the little stick
Whispers them to their places, and the steady drums
Draw them through the mazes of the dance.
They have raised their long sleeves, they have covered their eyes;
        Slowly their shrill voices
        Swell the steady song.

And the song said:
As a frightened bird whose love
Has wandered away from the nest,
I flutter my desolate wings.
For the wind blows back to my home,
And I long for my father's house.

Subtly from slender hips they swing,
Swaying, slanting delicately up and down.
And like the crimson mallow's flower
Glows their beauty, shedding flames afar.
They lift languid glances,
Peep distrustfully, till of a sudden
Ablaze with liquid light
Their soft eyes kindle. So dance to dance
Endlessly they weave, break off and dance again.
Now flutter their cuffs like a great bird in flight,
Now toss their long white sleeves like whirling snow.
So the hours go by, till now at last
The powder has blown from their cheeks, the black from their
    brows,
Flustered now are the fair faces, pins of pearl
Torn away, tangled the black tresses.
With combs they catch and gather in
The straying locks, put on the gossamer gown
That trailing winds about them, and in unison
Of body, song and dress, obedient
Each shadows each, as they glide softly to and fro.

FROM THE CHINESE OF CH'IN CHIA

To His Wife

Solemn, solemn the coachman gets ready to go;
'Chiang, chiang' the harness bells ring.
At break of dawn I must start on my long journey;
At cock-crow I must gird on my belt.
I turn back and look at the empty room;
For a moment I almost think I see you there.
One parting, but ten thousand regrets;

As I take my seat, my heart is unquiet.
What shall I do to tell you all my thoughts?
How can I let you know of all my love?
Precious hairpins make the head to shine
And bright mirrors can reflect beauty.
Fragrant herbs banish evil smells
And the scholar's lute has a clear note.
The man in the Book of Songs who was given a quince
Wanted to pay it back with precious stones.
When I think of all the things you have done for me,
How ashamed I am to have done so little for you!
Although I know that it is a poor return,
All I can give you is this description of my feelings.

FROM THE CHINESE OF TSO SSŬ

The Scholar in the Narrow Street

Flap, flap, the captive bird in the cage
Beating its wings against the four corners.
Sad and dreary, the scholar in the narrow street;
Clasping a shadow he dwells in an empty hut.
When he goes out, there is nowhere for him to go;
Thorns and brambles block his every path.
His plans are all discarded and come to nothing;
He is left stranded like a fish in a dry pond.
Without – he has not a single farthing of salary;
Within – there is not a peck of grain in his larder.
His relations all despise him for his lack of success;
Friends and companions grow daily more aloof.
Su Ch'in toured in triumph through the North,
Li Ssŭ rose to be Premier in the West;
With sudden splendour shone the flower of their fame,
With like swiftness it withered and decayed.
Though one drinks at a river, one cannot drink more than a
     belly-full;
Enough is good, but there is no use in satiety.
The bird in a forest can perch but on one bough,
And this should be the wise man's pattern.

FROM THE CHINESE OF CH'ÊN TZǓ-LUNG

The Little Cart

The little cart jolting and banging through the yellow haze of
dusk;
The man pushing behind, the woman pulling in front.
They have left the city and do not know where to go.
'Green, green, those elm-tree leaves; *they* will cure my hunger,
If only we could find some quiet place and sup on them together.'

The wind has flattened the yellow mother-wort;
Above it in the distance they see the walls of a house.
'There surely must be people living who'll give you something to
eat.'
They tap at the door, but no one comes; they look in, but the
kitchen is empty.
They stand hesitating in the lonely road and their tears fall like
rain.

FROM THE CHINESE OF LI-PO

I

'Last year we were fighting . . .'

Last year we were fighting at the source of the Sang-kan;
This year we are fighting on the Onion River road.
We have washed our swords in the surf of Parthian seas;
We have pastured our horses among the snows of the T'ien Shan,
The King's armies have grown grey and old
Fighting ten thousand leagues away from home.
The Huns have no trade but battle and carnage;
They have no fields or ploughlands,
But only wastes where white bones lie among yellow sands.
Where the House of Ch'in built the great wall that was to keep
away the Tartars.
There, in its turn, the House of Han lit beacons of war.
The beacons are always alight, fighting and marching never stop.
Men die in the field, slashing sword to sword;

The horses of the conquered neigh piteously to Heaven.
Crows and hawks peck for human guts,
Carry them in their beaks and hang them on the branches of
                                                    withered trees.
Captains and soldiers are smeared on the bushes and grass;
The General schemed in vain.
Know therefore that the sword is a cursed thing
Which the wise man uses only if he must.

2

'A foreign wind has stirred the horsemen of Tai'

A foreign wind has stirred the horsemen of Tai;
To the north they are blocking the pass of Lu-yang.
Weapons of Wu glint on the snowy lake;
From their march to the West will the soldiers ever come home?
They are half way over the Shang-liao Ford;
Blank and grim the yellow clouds hang.
An old mother is parting from her son,
She cries to heaven, standing in the wild scrub.
She gets through the banners to the captain on his white horse,
She clutches at him, and this is her mournful cry:
'*On the white poplar the autumn moon shines cold;*
Soon it will fall, in the hills of Yü-chang.
He whom you're taking was always a man of peace;
He was not trained to kill foreign foes.'
'Mother, I do not mind being killed in the fight;
For our sovereign's sake these monsters must be swept away.
When the soul is strong an arrow can plunge into a rock;
One must not shrink from things because they are hard.'
The towered ships soar like whales in flight;
The waves leap high in the Bay of the Fallen Star.
This song has a tune, but the tune cannot be played;
If the soldiers heard it, it would make their hair go grey.

F. SCOTT FITZGERALD
(1896–1940)

Voyelles

A black, E white, I red, U green, O blue, vowels
Some day I'll tell you where your genesis lies;
A – black velvet swarms of flies
Buzzing above the stench of voided bowels,
A gulf of shadow; E – where the iceberg rushes
White mists, tents, kings, shady strips;
I – purple, spilt blood, laughter of sweet lips
In anger – or the penitence of lushes;
U – cycle of time, rhythm of seas,
Peace of the paws of animals and wrinkles
On scholars' brows, strident tinkles;
O – the supreme trumpet note, peace
Of the spheres, of the angels. O equals
X-ray of her eyes; it equals sex.

BRIAN HILL
(b. 1896)

I

Spellbound

Black silhouettes in fog and snow
Against the oven vent-hole's glow,
    With rounded rumps,

Five children squat – poor little chaps!
Watching the baker as he slaps
    The bread and thumps

The heavy dough; his strong fists knead
The grey lumps into shapes to feed
    His oven shelf;

They hear the sizzling bread within;
The baker with a sweaty grin
    Hums to himself.

Small statues, they are crouched intent
Close to the red mouth of the vent,
    Warm as a breast;

And when for midnight feasts the bread
Comes crisp and shapely from its bed,
    Its cosy nest,

When underneath the smoky beams
From roll and crescent fragrance steams
    And crickets trill,

Then life itself breathes from that hole;
Under its rags each childish soul
    Is ravished till

It feels new strength surge up within –
Poor little Christs frost-nipped and thin!
    Each eager spy

Glues to the bars his small red nose,
Reciting what the oven shows
    His spellbound eye;

Quite stupefied, they kneel and pray
Bent down towards this kindly ray
    Of heaven's light.

They stoop so low their breeches split
And shirt-tails flutter from each slit
    In the cold night.

2

Under the Leaves the Wolf Howls

Under the leaves the wolf howls,
    Spewing up the feathery cushion
Gulped in his banquet of fowls;
    I consume myself, wolf-fashion.

Green things and fruit on the tree
    Are there for the reaching finger,
But the hedgerow spider – he
    With violets sates his hunger.

O to sleep! O to seethe and twist
    On Solomon's altar tables!
The broth spills over the rust
    And in Kedron's water bubbles.

MAURICE BOWRA
(b. 1898)

I

'You are always new . . .'

You are always new and always hidden;
More each day I yield to your desire.
But your love, hard-hearted friend, has bidden
Me to tests of iron and of fire.

You forbid my song, forbid my laughter,
Long ago you told me not to pray.
But I care not for what happens after
If from you I am not cast away.

From the earth and skies you would me sever;
I live, and my songs have ceased to swell.
'Tis as if to my free soul for ever
You had shut both Paradise and Hell.

2

'Is our time worse . . .'

Is our time worse than all the times that went before it,
Except that in the frenzy of its anxious grief
It touched the blackest of our sores and wished to cure it
But had no strength to bring relief?

There, in the West, Earth's sun still shines serene and steady,
And in its setting glow the roofs are glittering;
But here Death marks the houses with a cross already,
And calls the ravens on. Ravens are on the wing.

HORACE GREGORY
(b. 1898)

1

'Furius, Aurelius, . . .'

Furius, Aurelius, I'll work your own perversions
upon you and your persons, since you say my poems
prove that I'm effeminate, deep in homosexual vice.
A genuine poet must be chaste, industrious,
though his verse may give us
rich, voluptuous passion to please the
taste of those who read him and not only
delicate boys, but bearded men whose limbs are
stiff and out of practice. And you because my verses
contain many (thousands of) kisses, look at me
as though I were a girl. Come at me, and I'll be ready
to defile you and seduce you.

2

'Sweet girlish Thallus . . .'

Sweet girlish Thallus, as soft to your caresses as a little Spanish
    rabbit,
delicate as down plucked from a goose, and languid as the fallen
    member
that decorates an old man – but O, a hungry Thallus, covetous,
    rapacious,
eager as roaring waves or sea gulls with their beaks wide for food
    – O give me
back my cloak, my Spanish napkins, my ancient Bithynian tablets,
    that you are now displaying –
fool – to show these things in public as yours alone! Drop them,
    your fingers

thick with glue to capture all things. I'll sear you,
your pretty dainty little hips, your pretty hands, and I'll use
whips, inscribing phallus upon your flesh, O Thallus, broken,
    swaying,
lost in a violent storm, – little boat careering through a dark,
    angry ocean.

3

'When at last after long despair . . .'

When at last after long despair, our hopes ring true again
and long-starved desire eats, O then the mind leaps in the sunlight
    – Lesbia
so it was with me when you returned. Here was a treasure
more valuable than gold; you, whom I love beyond hope, giving
    yourself
to me again. That hour, a year of holidays, radiant,
where is the man more fortunate than I,
where can he find anything in life more glorious
than the sight of all his wealth restored?

VLADIMIR NABOKOV
(b. 1899)

FROM THE OLD RUSSIAN

The Song of Igor's Campaign

(lines 751–90)

IGOR'S ESCAPE
    Meanwhile, like an ermine,
    Igor has sped to the reeds,
    and [settled] upon the water
    like a white duck.
    He leapt upon the swift steed,
    and sprang off it,
    [and ran on], like a demon wolf,
    and sped to the meadowland of the Donets,
    and, like a falcon,
    flew up to the mists,
    killing geese
    and swans,
    for lunch,
    and for dinner,
    and for supper.

    And even as Igor, like a falcon, flew,
    Vlur, like a wolf, sped,
    shaking off by his passage the cold dew;
    for both had worn out
    their swift steeds.
    Says the Donets:
    'Prince Igor!
    Not small is your magnification,
    and Konchak's detestation,
    and the Russian land's gladness.'

    Igor says:
    'O Donets!

Not small is *your* magnification:
you it was who lolled
a prince on [your] waves;
who carpeted for him
with green grass
your silver banks;
who clothed him
with warm mists
under the shelter of the green tree;
who had him guarded
by the golden-eye on the water,
the gulls on the currents,
the [crested] black ducks on the winds.

ALLEN TATE
(b. 1899)

FROM THE LATIN (ANON.)

The Vigil of Venus

I

Tomorrow let loveless, let lover tomorrow make love:
O spring, singing spring, spring of the world renew!
In spring lovers consent and the birds marry
When the grove receives in her hair the nuptial dew.

Tomorrow may loveless, may lover tomorrow make love.

II

Tomorrow's the day when the prime Zeus made love:
Out of lightning foam shot deep in the heaving sea
(Witnessed by green crowds of finny horses)
Dione rising and falling, he made to be!

Tomorrow may loveless, may lover tomorrow make love.

III

Tomorrow the Joiner of love in the gracious shade
Twines her green huts with boughs of myrtle claws,
Tomorrow leads her gangs to the singing woods:
Tomorrow Dione, on high, lays down the laws.

Tomorrow may loveless, may lover tomorrow make love.

IV

She shines the tarnished year with glowing buds
That, wakening, head up to the western wind

In eager clusters. Goddess! You deign to scatter
Lucent night-drip of dew; for you are kind.

    Tomorrow may loveless, may lover tomorrow make love.

V

The heavy teardrops stretch, ready to fall,
Then falls each glistening bead to the earth beneath:
The moisture that the serene stars sent down
Loosens the virgin bud from the sliding sheath.

    Tomorrow may loveless, may lover tomorrow make love.

VI

Look, the high crimsons have revealed their shame.
The burning rose turns in her secret bed,
The goddess has bidden the girdle to loose its folds
That the rose at dawn may give her maidenhead.

    Tomorrow may loveless, may lover tomorrow make love.

VII

The blood of Venus enters her blood, Love's kiss
Has made the drowsy virgin modestly bold;
Tomorrow the bride is not ashamed to take
The burning taper from its hidden fold.

    Tomorrow may loveless, may lover tomorrow make love.

VIII

The goddess herself has sent nymphs to the woods,
The Boy with girls to the myrtles; perhaps you think
That Love's not truly tame if he shows his arrows?
Go, girls! Unarmed, Love beckons. You must not shrink.

    Tomorrow may loveless, may lover tomorrow make love.

IX

Bidden unarmed to go and to go naked
Lest he destroy with bow, with dart, with brand –
Yet, girls, Cupid is pretty, and you must know
That Love unarmed can pierce with naked hand!

Tomorrow may loveless, may lover tomorrow make love.

X

Here will be girls of the farm and girls of the mountain
And girls who live by forest, or grove, or spring.
The mother of the Flying Boy has smiled
And said: Now, girls, beware his naked sting!

Tomorrow may loveless, may lover tomorrow make love.

XI

Gently she asks may she bend virginity?
Gently that you, a modest girl, may yield.
Now, should you come, for three nights you would see
Delirious bands in every grove and field.

Tomorrow may loveless, may lover tomorrow make love.

XII

Venus herself has maidens as pure as you;
So, Delia, one thing only we ask: Go away!
That the wood shall not be bloody with slaughtered beasts
When Venus flicks the shadows with greening spray.

Tomorrow may loveless, may lover tomorrow make love.

XIII

Among the garlands, among the myrtle bowers
Ceres and Bacchus, and the god of verse, delay.

Nightlong the watch must be kept with votive cry –
Dione's queen of the woods: Diana, make way!

Tomorrow may loveless, may lover tomorrow make love.

XIV

She places her court among the flowers of Hybla;
Presiding, she speaks her laws; the Graces are near.
Hybla, give all your blossoms, and bring, Hybla,
The brightest plain of Enna for the whole year.

Tomorrow may loveless, may lover tomorrow make love.

XV

With spring the father-sky remakes the world:
The male shower has flowed into the bride,
Earth's body; then shifted through sky and sea and land
To touch the quickening child in her deep side.

Tomorrow may loveless, may lover tomorrow make love.

XVI

Over sky and land and down under the sea
On the path of the seed the goddess brought to earth
And dropped into our veins created fire,
That men might know the mysteries of birth.

Tomorrow may loveless, may lover tomorrow make love.

XVII

Body and mind the inventive Creatress fills
With spirit blowing its invariable power:
The Sabine girls she gave to the sons of Rome
And sowed the seed exiled from the Trojan tower.

Tomorrow may loveless, may lover tomorrow make love.

XVIII

Lavinia of Laurentum she chose to bed
Her son Aeneas, and for the black Mars won
The virgin Silvia, to found the Roman line:
Sire Romulus, and Caesar her grandson.

Tomorrow may loveless, may lover tomorrow make love.

XIX

Venus knows country matters: country knows Venus:
For Love, Dione's boy, was born on the farm.
From the rich furrow she snatched him to her breast,
With tender flowers taught him peculiar charm.

Tomorrow may loveless, may lover tomorrow make love.

XX

See how the bullocks rub their flanks with broom!
See the ram pursue through the shade the bleating ewe,
For lovers' union is Venus in kind pursuit;
And she tells the birds to forget their winter woe.

Tomorrow may loveless, may lover tomorrow make love.

XXI

Now the tall swans with hoarse cries thrash the lake:
The girl of Tereus pours from the poplar ring
Musical change – sad sister who bewails
Her act of darkness with the barbarous king!

Tomorrow may loveless, may lover tomorrow make love.

XXII

She sings, we are silent. When will my spring come?
Shall I find my voice when I shall be as the swallow?
Silence destroyed the Amyclae: they were dumb.
Silent, I lost the muse. Return, Apollo!

Tomorrow let loveless, let lover tomorrow make love.

BASIL BUNTING
(b. 1900)

IMITATIONS FROM FRANÇOIS VILLON

I

'Remember, imbeciles and wits'

Remember, imbeciles and wits,
Scots and ascetics, fair and foul,
Young girls with little tender tits,
That DEATH is written over all.

Worn hides that scarcely clothe the soul
They are so rotten, old and thin,
Or firm and soft and warm and full –
Fellmonger Death gets every skin.

All that is piteous, all that's fair,
All that is fat and scant of breath,
Elisha's baldness, Helen's hair,
Is Death's collateral:

Three score and ten years after sight
Of this pay me your pulse and breath
Value received. And who dare cite,
As we forgive our debtors, Death?

Abélard and Éloïse,
Henry the Fowler, Charlemagne,
Genée, Lopokova, all these
Die, die in pain.

And General Grant and General Lee,
Patti and Florence Nightingale,
Like Tyro and Antiope
Drift among ghosts in Hell,

Know nothing, are nothing, save a fume
Driving across a mind

Preoccupied with this: Our doom
Is, to be sifted by the wind,

Heaped up, smoothed down like silly sands.
We are less permanent than thought.
The Emperor with the Golden Hands

Is still a word, a tint, a tone,
Insubstantial-glorious,
When we ourselves are dead and gone
And the green grass growing over us.

2

'Let his days be few . . .'

Let his days be few and let
His bishoprick pass to another,
For he fed me on carrion and on a dry crust,
Mouldy bread that his dog had vomited,
I lying on my back in the dark place, in the grave,
Fettered to a post in the damp cellarage.
    Whereinall we differ not. But they have swept the floor,
There are no dancers, no somersaulters now,
Only bricks and bleak black cement and bricks,
Only the military tread and the snap of the locks.
    Mine was a threeplank bed whereon
I lay and cursed the weary sun.
They took away the prison clothes
And on the frosty nights I froze.
I had a Bible where I read
That Jesus came to raise the dead –
I kept myself from going mad
By singing an old bawdy ballad
And birds sang on my windowsill
And tortured me till I was ill,
But Archipiada came to me
And comforted my cold body
And Circe excellent utterer of her mind

Lay with me in that dungeon for a year
Making a silk purse from an old sow's ear
Till Ronsard put a thimble on her tongue.
   Whereinall we differ not. But they have named all the stars,
Trodden down the scrub of the desert, run the white moon to a
      schedule,
Joshua's serf whose beauty drove men mad.
They have melted the snows from Erebus, weighed the clouds,
Hunted down the white bear, hunted the whale the seal the
      kangaroo,
They have sent private enquiry agents onto Archipiada:
What is your name? Your maiden name?
Go in there to be searched. I suspect it is not your true name.
Distinguishing marks if any? (O anthropometrics!)
Now the thumbprints for filing.
Colour of hair? of eyes? of hands? O Bertillon!
How many golden prints on the smudgy page?

ROY CAMPBELL

(1902–1957)

FROM THE FRENCH OF CHARLES BAUDELAIRE

I

The Albatross

Sometimes for sport the men of loafing crews
Snare the great albatrosses of the deep,
The indolent companions of their cruise
As through the bitter vastitudes they sweep.

Scarce have they fished aboard these airy kings
When helpless on such unaccustomed floors,
They piteously drop their huge white wings
And trail them at their sides like drifting oars.

How comical, how ugly, and how meek
Appears this soarer of celestial snows!
One, with his pipe, teases the golden beak,
One limping, mocks the cripple as he goes.

The Poet, like this monarch of the clouds,
Despising archers, rides the storm elate.
But, stranded on the earth to jeering crowds,
The great wings of the giant baulk his gait.

2

Ill Luck

So huge a burden to support
Your courage, Sisyphus, would ask;
Well though my heart attacks its task,
Yet Art is long and Time is short.

Far from the famed memorial arch
Towards a lonely grave I come.

My heart in its funereal march
Goes beating like a muffled drum.

– Yet many a gem lies hidden still
Of whom no pick-axe, spade, or drill
The lonely secrecy invades;

And many a flower, to heal regret,
Pours forth its fragrant secret yet
Amidst the solitary shades.

3

The Giantess

Of old when Nature, in her verve defiant,
Conceived each day some birth of monstrous mien,
I would have lived near some young female giant
Like a voluptuous cat beside a queen;

To see her body flowering with her soul
Freely develop in her mighty games,
And in the mists that through her gaze would roll
Guess that her heart was hatching sombre flames;

To roam her mighty contours as I please,
Ramp on the cliff of her tremendous knees,
And in the solstice, when the suns that kill

Make her stretch out across the land and rest,
To sleep beneath the shadow of her breast
Like a hushed village underneath a hill.

4

'With waving opalescence in her gown'

With waving opalescence in her gown,
Even when she walks along, you think she's dancing,
Like those long snakes which charmers, while entrancing,
Wave with their wands, in cadence, up and down.

Like the sad sands of deserts and their skies,
By human sufferings untouched and free,
Or like the surfy curtains of the sea,
She flaunts a cold indifference. Her eyes

Are made of charming minerals well-burnished.
Her nature, both by sphinx and angel furnished,
Is old, intact, symbolic, and bizarre:

She seems, made all of gems, steel, light, and gold,
In barrenness, majestic, hard, and cold,
To blaze forever, like a useless star.

5

The Carcase

The object that we saw, let us recall,
This summer morn when warmth and beauty mingle –
At the path's turn, a carcase lay asprawl
     Upon a bed of shingle.

Legs raised, like some old whore far-gone in passion,
The burning, deadly, poison-sweating mass
Opened its paunch in careless, cynic fashion,
     Ballooned with evil gas.

On this putrescence the sun blazed in gold,
Cooking it to a turn with eager care –
So to repay to Nature, hundredfold,
     What she had mingled there.

The sky, as on the opening of a flower,
On this superb obscenity smiled bright.
The stench drove at us, with such fearsome power
     You thought you'd swoon outright.

Flies trumpeted upon the rotten belly
Whence larvae poured in legions far and wide,
And flowed, like molten and liquescent jelly,
     Down living rags of hide.

The mass ran down, or, like a wave elated
Rolled itself on, and crackled as if frying:
You'd think that corpse, by vague breath animated,
    Drew life from multiplying.

Through that strange world a rustling rumour ran
Like rushing water or a gust of air;
Or grain that winnowers, with rhythmic fan,
    Sweep simmering here and there.

It seemed a dream after the forms grew fainter,
Or like a sketch that slowly seems to dawn
On a forgotten canvas, which the painter
    From memory has drawn.

Behind the rocks a restless cur that slunk
Eyed us with fretful greed to recommence
His feast, amidst the bonework, on the chunk
    That he had torn from thence.

Yet you'll resemble this infection too
One day, and stink and sprawl in such a fashion,
Star of my eyes, sun of my nature, you,
    My angel and my passion!

Yes, you must come to this, O queen of graces,
At length, when the last sacraments are over,
And you go down to moulder in dark places
    Beneath the grass and clover.

Then tell the vermin as it takes its pleasance
And feasts with kisses on that face of yours,
I've kept intact in form and godlike essence
    Our decomposed amours!

6

Meditation

    Be good, my Sorrow: hush now: settle down.
    You sighed for dusk, and now it comes: look there!

A denser atmosphere obscures the town,
To some restoring peace, to others care.

While the lewd multitude, like hungry beasts,
By pleasure scourged (no thug so fierce as he!)
Go forth to seek remorse among their feasts —
Come, take my hand; escape from them with me.

From balconies of sky, around us yet,
Lean the dead years in fashions that have ceased.
Out of the depth of waters smiles Regret.

The sun sinks moribund beneath an arch,
And like a long shroud rustling from the East,
Hark, Love, the gentle Night is on the march.

FROM THE SPANISH OF ST JOHN OF THE CROSS

I

'*Upon a gloomy night*'

(Song of the soul in rapture at having arrived at the height of perfection,
which is union with God by the road of spiritual negation)

Upon a gloomy night,
With all my cares to loving ardours flushed,
(O venture of delight!)
With nobody in sight
I went abroad when all my house was hushed.

In safety, in disguise,
In darkness up the secret stair I crept,
(O happy enterprise)
Concealed from other eyes
When all my house at length in silence slept.

Upon that lucky night
In secrecy, inscrutable to sight,
I went without discerning
And with no other light
Except for that which in my heart was burning.

It lit and led me through
More certain than the light of noonday clear
To where One waited near
Whose presence well I knew,
There where no other presence might appear.

Oh night that was my guide!
Oh darkness dearer than the morning's pride,
Oh night that joined the lover
To the beloved bride
Transfiguring them each into the other.

Within my flowering breast
Which only for himself entire I save
He sank into his rest
And all my gifts I gave
Lulled by the airs with which the cedars wave.

Over the ramparts fanned
While the fresh wind was fluttering his tresses,
With his serenest hand
My neck he wounded, and
Suspended every sense with its caresses.

Lost to myself I stayed
My face upon my lover having laid
From all endeavour ceasing:
And all my cares releasing
Threw them amongst the lilies there to fade.

2

Song of the soul that is glad to know God by faith

How well I know that fountain's rushing flow
Although by night

Its deathless spring is hidden. Even so
Full well I guess from whence its sources flow
Though it be night.

Its origin (since it has none) none knows:
But that all origin from it arose
Although by night.

I know there is no other thing so fair
And earth and heaven drink refreshment there
Although by night.

Full well I know its depth no man can sound
And that no ford to cross it can be found
Though it be night

Its clarity unclouded still shall be:
Out of it comes the light by which we see
Though it be night.

Flush with its banks the stream so proudly swells;
I know it waters nations, heavens, and hells
Though it be night.

The current that is nourished by this source
I know to be omnipotent in force
Although by night.

From source and current a new current swells
Which neither of the other twain excels
Though it be night.

The eternal source hides in the Living Bread
That we with life eternal may be fed
Though it be night.

Here to all creatures it is crying, hark!
That they should drink their fill though in the dark,
For it is night.

This living fount which is to me so dear
Within the bread of life I see it clear
Though it be night.

FROM THE SPANISH OF FEDERICO GARCIA LORCA

I

Romance of the Civil Guard of Spain

Their horses are as black as night
Upon whose hoofs black horseshoes clink;
Upon their cloaks, with dismal sheen,
Shine smears of wax and ink.
The reason why they cannot weep
Is that their skulls are full of lead.
With souls of patent leather
Along the roads they tread.
Hunchbacked and nocturnal,
You feel when they're at hand
Silences of india-rubber
And fears like grains of sand.
They travel where they like,
Concealing in their skulls of neuters
A blurred astronomy of pistols
And shadowy six-shooters.

O city of the gipsy people!
Flags at the corners of the streets.
With calabashes and the moon
And cherries candied into sweets.
O city of the gipsy people!
Who can forget you who has seen?
City of sorrow and of musk
With towers of cinnamon between.
When the night-time has arrived,
The night-time of the night,
Gipsy folk upon their anvils
Are forging suns and darts of light.
A wounded horse arrives and runs
To all the doors with plaintive whine.
Cocks of glass are crowing loud
At Jerez of the Frontier-Line.
Around the corner of surprise

The wind bursts naked on the sight,
In the night, the silver night-time,
In the night-time of the night.

2

Reyerta

In the midst of the ravine,
Glinting Albacete blades,
Beautified with rival bloods
Flash like fishes in the shades.
A hard flat light of playing cards
Outlines, against the bitter green,
Shapes of infuriated horses
And profiles of equestrian mien.
Under the branches of an olive,
Weep two women bent with age,
While the bull of altercation
Clambers up the walls with rage.
Black angels come with handkerchiefs
And water from the snowline-boulders,
Angels with vast wings, like the blades
Of Albacete, on their shoulders,
Juan Antonio from Montilla
Down the slope goes rolling dead,
With his flesh stuck full of lilies,
A sliced pomegranate for his head;
And now the cross of fire ascends
Along the highways of the dead.
The Judge and Civil Guard their way
Along the olive orchard take,
Where slithered blood begins to moan
The dumb song of an injured snake.
'Gentleman of the Civil Guard!
The same old story as before –
Five of the Carthaginians slain
And of the Roman people four.'

The maddening afternoon of figtrees
And of hot rumours, ending soon,
Fell down between the wounded thighs
Of the wild horsemen, in a swoon.
Black angels fly across the air
From which the setting sun departs,
Angels with long dark streaming hair
And oil of olives in their hearts.

3

Somnambulistic Ballad

Green, green, how deeply green!
Green the wind and green the bough,
The ship upon the ocean seen,
The horse upon the mountain's brow.
With the shadows round her waist
Upon her balcony she dreams.
Green her flesh and green her tresses,
In her eyes chill silver gleams.
Green, green, how deeply green,
While the gipsy moonbeam plays
Things at her are gazing keenly
But she cannot meet their gaze.

Green, green, how deeply green!
See the great stars of the frost
Come rustling with the fish of shadow
To find the way the dawn has lost.
The figtree chafes the passing wind
With the sandpaper of its leaves,
And hissing like a thievish cat,
With bristled fur, the mountain heaves.
But who will come? And by what path?
On her verandah lingers she,
Green her flesh and green her hair,
Dreaming of the bitter sea.

'Companion, I should like to trade
My pony for your house and grange,
To swap my saddle for your mirror,
My sheath-knife for your rug to change.'
'Companion, I have galloped bleeding
From Cabra's passes down the range.'
'If it could be arranged, my lad,
I'd clinch the bargain; but you see
Now I am no longer I,
Nor does my house belong to me.'
'Companion, I should like to die
Respectably at home in bed,
A bed of steel if possible,
With sheets of linen smoothly spread.
Can you not see this gash I carry
From rib to throat, from chin to chest?'
'Three hundred roses darkly red
Spatter the white front of your vest.
Your blood comes oozing out to spread,
Around your sash, its ghostly smell.
But now I am no longer I
Nor is my house my own to sell.'
'Let me go up tonight at least,
And climb the dim verandah's height.
Let me go up! O let me climb
To the verandah green with light!
O chill verandahs of the moon
Whence fall the waters of the night!'

And now the two companions climb
Up where the high verandah sheers,
Leaving a little track of blood
Leaving a little trail of tears.
Trembling along the roofs, a thousand
Sparkles of tin reflect the ray.
A thousand tambourines of glass
Wounded the dawning of the day.

Green, green, how deeply green!
Green the wind and green the bough.

The two companions clambered up
And a long wind began to sough
Which left upon the mouth a savour
Of gall and mint and basil-flowers.
'Companion! Tell me. Where is she?
Where is that bitter girl of ours?'
'How many times she waited for you!
How long she waited, hoped, and sighed,
Fresh her face, and black her tresses,
Upon this green verandah-side!'

Over the surface of the pond
The body of the gipsy sways.
Green her flesh, and green her tresses,
Her eyes a frosty silver glaze.
An icicle hung from the moon
Suspends her from the water there.
The night became as intimate
As if it were the village square.
The drunkards of the Civil Guard
Banging the door, began to swear.
Green, O green, how deeply green!
Green the wind and green the bough,
The ship upon the waters seen,
The horse upon the mountain's brow.

4

Song of the Horseman

Córdoba.
Remote and lonely.

Jet-black mare and full round moon,
With olives in my saddle bags,
Although I know the road so well
I shall not get to Córdoba.

Across the plain, across the wind,
Jet-black mare and full red moon,

Death is gazing down upon me,
Down from the towers of Córdoba.

Ay! The road so dark and long.
Ay! My mare so tired yet brave.
Death is waiting for me there
Before I get to Córdoba.

Córdoba.
Remote and lonely.

FROM THE PORTUGUESE OF LUIS DE CAMÕES

On a Shipmate, Pero Moniz, dying at Sea

My years on earth were short, but long for me,
And full of bitter hardship at the best:
My light of day sinks early in the sea:
Five lustres from my birth I took my rest.
Through distant lands and seas I was a ranger
Seeking some cure or remedy for life,
Which he whom Fortune loves not as a wife,
Will seek in vain through strife, and toil, and danger.
Portugal reared me in my green, my darling
Alanguer, but the dank, corrupted air
That festers in the marshes around there
Has made me food for fish here in the snarling,
Fierce seas that dark the Abyssinian shore,
Far from the happy homeland I adore.

FROM THE PORTUGUESE OF JOSÉ RÉGIO

Yes, I sing – Fado Canção

Yes, I sing.
It is my destiny.
But I sing as a child screams

Who clings to the balcony
Of a building that's on fire,
In which he is left forgotten . . .
The square, beneath, is empty.
The sky, above, is hidden.
The balcony is dizzily high;
The ladders are turned to dust and ashes.
The crazy floor is crumbling.
The scream of anguish alone
Pierces an echo in the distance . . .
And no one comes to his rescue.
I know that no one is coming,
No one at all.
The solitude, of which I'm dying,
Lends me a helping hand,
And exchanges a look of kindness
Which saves me from my panic . . .
But how much the better I know
And how much more devoutly believe in
That echo that sounds in the distance . . .

So the louder and better I sing!

FROM THE PORTUGUESE OF PACO D'ARCOS

I

Fear

Fear is not dread of pirates on the river
Nor of the sea's typhoons.
It's not the dread of firing in the night
On the river thronged with treachery and junks.
It's not the dread of hanged men seen
In the white moonlight,
In the forest of mangoes of the Black Sand.
Fear's not the dread of hunger, war, or plague,
Nor of the lepers' scabs on Saint John's Island.
It is not the suspicion

That death is stalking us
Continually
And in the end will carry us away.

Fear is not the contagion of sorrow
When evening falls
And the sunset stains with blood
The muddy seashore,
The lands, and the sky,
Until these isles are swallowed up in shade
And the peaks in darkness
And nothing is left save the shadows
And cries traverse the night,
Coming from I know not whence,
Going I know not whither.

Fear is not dread of traps
Or daggers
Or of red kisses that betray
And slowly suck our lives . . .

Fear is the dread that you might go
And leave me here alone.

2

*Febrile City between the Mountain and the Sea —
Rio de Janeiro*

Curved and recurved,
The curves of the bay
Pass and escape,
Undulate and glide
Between the mountain and the sea.

Sad mountain, sad black mountain
With all your torpid mildness.
Sea of flat calm,
Sea for tiny children,
Sea without storms or shipwrecks,

With nothing but the smoke of steamers, warm evenings
And the very white moonlight in quiet nights.

This febrile city between the sea and the mountain.
All the perfidious spirit of the town
Fits with the destiny that soldered it
To the dark mountain and the silver sea.
All its charm derives from this strife,
All its weakness and all its strength.
It fears that the mountain might crush it down
And that the sea might engulf it.

Curved and recurved,
The curves of the bay
Pass and escape,
Undulate and glide
Between the mountain and the sea.

The town melts into the mountain,
The bay melts into the night;
But in me nothing melts into anything –
Neither into regret,
Nor desire,
Nor my flesh into your flesh,
Nor my shadow into your shadow.

JAMES BLAIR LEISHMAN
(1902–1963)

FROM THE LATIN OF HORACE

To Bandusia

(*Odes*, Book III, 13)
HIS SABINE SPRING

Hail, Bandusia, hail, more than crystalline spring,
well-deserving of sweet wine and of flowers strown,
      you tomorrow a firstling
    kid shall honour, with budding horns

deemed foretellers of one famous in love and war –
ah, but vainly, for your coolly-pellucid waves
      soon this child of the wanton
    flock shall stain with a darker hue.

You, when blazing in fierce splendour the Dog-star reigns,
flow intangibly on, proffer unfailingly
      oxen weary with ploughing,
    roaming flocks, a delicious chill.

You too men shall account one of the nobler springs,
while these verses of mine tell of the ilex-tree
      overhanging the grotto
    whence your chattering waters leap.

JOHN MICHAEL COHEN
(b. 1903)

I

'It may occur . . .'

It may occur in one way or another,
but there's a certain, there's a fatal hour,
blacker than monks, more stifling than the clergy,
when we are overtaken by insanity.

Frost. And the night outside the window's watching
conventionally the coldness of the ice.
In its furcoat and armchair the Soul's purring
the same thing all the time and on and on.

And the relief and contour of a twig,
the poker's shadow and the parquet floor
out of remorse and dreaming mould the sinful
snowstorm that blows right through the day and night.

The night is still. The night is clear and frosty;
like a blind puppy lapping up its milk,
midst all the unconscious darkness of the spruces
the palings drink the radiance of the stars.

It might drip from the firs, they might be flickering,
it might be night was guttering with wax.
Fir after fir the snow blinds with its paw and
on the hollow tree's another's silhouette.

It might be that the tall sky and the quiet,
the elegiac waves of the telegraph,
were expectation, stood for the cry: 'Answer!'
or were the echo of another quiet.

It might be dumb, that view of twigs and needles,
and the other view, up there, be hard of hearing,

and the path sparkling on the slopes be answer
to some 'Hullo' that somebody had shouted.

Frost. And the night outside the window's watching
conventionally the coldness of the ice.
In its furcoat and armchair the Soul's purring
the same thing all the time and on and on.

Oh lips, oh lips! He's pressed them till they bleed.
He's put his arms across his face. He's trembling.
For his biographer this chalk white, deathly
motive calls up whirlwinds of speculation.

2

Spasskoye

This memorable September crumbles upon Spasskoye.
Is it not time today to leave the cottage?
Beyond the fence echoes the shepherd's call
and in the woods you've heard the axe's stroke.

Last night beyond the park the marsh was shivering.
The sun no sooner rose than it was gone.
No harebell now drinks the rheumatic dews
and dirty lilac dropsy coats the birches.

The sad wood needs a rest beneath the snow
in the eternal slumber of the bear-dens.
Amidst the stumps within the blackened fences
the columned park gapes like a full obituary.

The birchgrove has not ceased to fade and smudge,
to cast its aqueous shade and to grow thin.
That is grumbling still, and you're fifteen again,
and once more – Oh my boy, where shall we put them all?

Already they're as many – it's no joke –
as birds in the bushes, mushrooms by the hedge.
They were already veiling the horizon;
now with their mist they've overcast a new one.

On the night of his death from typhus the feverish clown
hears a roar, 'the Gods'' Homeric laughter.
Now the same agony in remote Spasskoye
views in its wandering mind the timber house.

DUDLEY FITTS
(b. 1903)

FROM THE GREEK OF LEONIDAS

Cold Pastoral

Homeward at evening through the drifted snow
The cows plod back to shelter from the hill;
But ah, the long strange sleep
Of the cow-herd Therimachos lying beneath the oak,
Struck still, still, by the fire that falls from heaven!

FROM THE GREEK OF PARMENION

On the Dead at Thermopylai

Him who, altering the ways of earth and sea,
Sailed on the land and made his march on the water,
Him the valour of three hundred Spartan spears hurled back.

Be ashamed O mountains and sea!

FROM THE GREEK OF ASKLEPIADES

To Zeus of the Rains

Rain at night and the north wind whirling
And wine and the stumbling loneliness:
Moschos my fair love!
I cried . . .

       (Trudge on, on, and never a friendly door
       Down all the long street . . .)
I cried
Dripping with rain:

       No end, O Zeus?
Dear Zeus, be gentle! Were you not once in love?

FROM THE GREEK OF LEONIDAS OF TARENTUM

Epitaph of a Sailor

These were my end: a fierce down-squall from the east,
And night, and the waves of Orion's stormy setting:
And I, Kallaischros, yielded my life
Far on the waste of the lonely Libyan sea.
And now I roll with drifting currents, the prey
Of fishes:

        and this gravestone lies
If it says that it marks the place of my burial.

FROM THE GREEK OF SOPHOCLES

(with Robert Fitzgerald)

Antigone

ODE I

CHORUS: *[Strophe 1*

Numberless are the world's wonders, but none
More wonderful than man; the stormgray sea
Yields to his prows, the huge crests bear him high;
Earth, holy and inexhaustible, is graven
With shining furrows where his plows have gone
Year after year, the timeless labor of stallions.

                                      [Antistrophe 1

The lightboned birds and beasts that cling to cover,
The lithe fish lighting their reaches of dim water,
All are taken, tamed in the net of his mind;
The lion on the hill, the wild horse windy-maned,
Resign to him; and his blunt yoke has broken
The sultry shoulders of the mountain bull.

                                      [Strophe 2

Words also, and thought as rapid as air,
He fashions to his good use; statecraft is his,
And his the skill that deflects the arrows of snow,

The spears of winter rain: from every wind
He has made himself secure – from all but one:
In the late wind of death he cannot stand.

[*Antistrophe* 2

O clear intelligence, force beyond all measure!
O fate of man, working both good and evil!
When the laws are kept, how proudly his city stands!
When the laws are broken, what of his city then?
Never may the anárchic man find rest at my hearth,
Never be it said that my thoughts are his thoughts.

FRANK O'CONNOR
(1903–1966)

The Scholar and the Cat

Each of us pursues his trade,
I and Pangur my comrade,
His whole fancy on the hunt,
And mine for learning ardent.

More than fame I love to be
Among my books and study,
Pangur does not grudge me it,
Content with his own merit.

When – a heavenly time! – we are
In our small room together
Each of us has his own sport
And asks no greater comfort.

While he sets his round sharp eye
On the wall of my study
I turn mine, though lost its edge
On the great wall of knowledge.

Now a mouse drops in his net
After some mighty onset
While into my bag I cram
Some difficult darksome problem.

When a mouse comes to the kill
Pangur exults, a marvel!
I have when some secret's won
My hour of exultation.

Though we work for days and years
Neither the other hinders;

Each is competent and hence
Enjoys his skill in silence.

Master of the death of mice,
He keeps in daily practice,
I too, making dark things clear,
Am of my trade a master.

2

The Sweetness of Nature

Endlessly over the water
    Birds of the Bann are singing;
Sweeter to me their voices
    Than any churchbell's ringing.

Over the plain of Moyra
    Under the heels of foemen
I saw my people broken
    As flax is scutched by women.

But the cries I hear by Derry
    Are not of men triumphant;
I hear their calls in the evening,
    Swans calm and exultant.

I hear the stag's belling
    Over the valley's steepness;
No music on the earth
    Can move me like its sweetness.

Christ, Christ hear me!
    Christ, Christ of Thy meekness!
Christ, Christ love me!
    Sever me not from Thy sweetness!

3

May

May's the merriest time of all,
    Life comes back to everything,

While a ray of light remains
    The never weary blackbirds sing.

That's the cuckoo's strident voice,
    'Welcome summer great and good!'
All the fury of the storm
    Lost in tangles of the wood.

Summer stems the languid stream,
    Thirsty horses rush the pool,
Bracken bristles everywhere,
    White bog-cotton is in bloom.

Scant of breath the burdened bees
    Carry home the flowery spoil,
To the mountains go the cows,
    The ant is glutted with his meal.

The wind awakes the woodland's harp,
    The sail falls and the world's at rest,
A mist of heat upon the hills
    And the water full of mist.

The corncrake drones, a bustling bard,
    The cold cascade that leaps the rock
Sings of the snugness of the pool,
    Their season come, the rushes talk.

The man grows strong, the virgin tall,
    Each in his glory, firm and light,
Bright the far and fertile plain,
    Bright the wood from floor to height.

Here among the meadowlands
    An eager flock of birds descends,
And there a stream runs white and fast
    Where the murmuring meadow bends.

And you long to race a horse
    Headlong through the parting crowd,
The sun has scarcely touched the land
    But the water-flags are gold.

Frightened, foolish, frail, a bird
    Sings of it with throbbing breast –
The lark that flings its praise abroad,
    May the brightest and the best.

4

Caoilte

Winter time is bleak, the wind
    Drives the stag from height to height;
Belling at the mountain's cold
    Untameable he strays tonight.

The old stag of Carran scarce
    Dare sleep within his den,
While the stag of Aughty hears
    Wolves call in every glen.

Long ago Osgar and I
    And Diarmuid heard that cry;
And we listened to the wolves
    As the frosty night went by.

Now the stag that's filled with sleep
    Lays his lordly side to rest
As if earth had drawn him down
    To the winter's icy breast.

Though I drowse above the fire
    Many a winter morning drear
My hand was tight about a sword
    A battleaxe or spear.

And though I sleep cold tonight,
    God, I offer thanks to you
And to Christ, the Virgin's Son,
    For the mighty men I slew.

5

The King of Connacht

'Have you seen Hugh,
    The Connacht king in the field?'
'All that we saw
    Was his shadow under his shield.'

6

Liadain

Gain without gladness
    Is in the bargain I have struck;
One that I loved I wrought to madness.

Mad beyond measure
    But for God's fear that numbed her heart
She that would not do his pleasure.

Was it so great
    My treason? Was I not always kind?
Why should it turn his love to hate?

Liadain,
    That is my name, and Curithir
The man I loved; you know my sin.

Alas too fleet!
    Too brief my pleasure at his side;
With him the passionate hours were sweet.

Woods woke
    About us for a lullaby,
And the blue waves in music spoke.

And now too late
    More than for all my sins I grieve
That I turned his love to hate.

Why should I hide
    That he is still my heart's desire
More than all the world beside?

A furnace blast
    Of love has melted down my heart,
Without his love it cannot last.

7

Fathers and Sons

Young at his father's fire
    He lords it and takes the best;
Old, at the fire of his son,
    He covers his knees with his breast.

Father and son take shares?
    The son the father devours!
All that is ours is theirs,
    Nothing of theirs is ours.

FROM THE IRISH OF MURROUGH O'DALY

On the Death of His Wife

I parted from my life last night,
    A woman's body sunk in clay:
The tender bosom that I loved
    Wrapped in a sheet they took away.

The heavy blossom that had lit
    The ancient boughs is tossed and blown;
Hers was the burden of delight
    That long had weighed the old tree down.

And I am left alone tonight
    And desolate is the world I see
For lovely was that woman's weight
    That even last night had lain on me.

Weeping I look upon the place
    Where she used to rest her head –
For yesterday her body's length
    Reposed upon you too, my bed.

Yesterday that smiling face
  Upon one side of you was laid
That could match the hazel bloom
  In its dark delicate sweet shade.

Maelva of the shadowy brows
  Was the mead-cask at my side;
Fairest of all flowers that grow
  Was the beauty that has died.

My body's self deserts me now,
  The half of me that was her own,
Since all I knew of brightness died
  Half of me lingers, half is gone.

The face that was like hawthorn bloom
  Was my right foot and my right side;
And my right hand and my right eye
  Were no more mine than hers who died.

Poor is the share of me that's left
  Since half of me died with my wife;
I shudder at the words I speak;
  Dear God, that girl was half my life.

And our first look was her first love;
  No man had fondled ere I came
The little breasts so small and firm
  And the long body like a flame.

For twenty years we shared a home,
  Our converse milder with each year;
Eleven children in its time
  Did that tall stately body bear.

It was the King of hosts and roads
  Who snatched her from me in her prime:
Little she wished to leave alone
  The man she loved before her time.

Now King of churches and of bells,
  Though never raised to pledge a lie
That woman's hand – can it be true? –
  No more beneath my head will lie.

HAROLD ACTON
(b. 1904)

Earthquake

The earth revives,
All beings tremble,
But this is only for a second,
Then all is hushed.

There is silence after the heave,
A silence like annihilation,
Sunshine smiles to the children,
To the dazed and terrified children.

I remember this once happened in my youth,
Mother told me 'twas an enormous turtle opening and shutting its
    eyes.
Under the earth is there truly a giant turtle?
I saw it with the eye of a youthful mind.

Now the enormous turtle is dead
And yet I see it soaring through the air.
I know that the quake was caused by a volcano
But how does this knowledge benefit my soul?

FROM THE CHINESE OF PIEN CHIH-LIN
Friend and Cigarettes

Please smoke, take another.
I still can remember that you used to say the *White and Gold Dragon*
had a delicate and subtle flavour.
And I asked you if the flavour was like memories.
I feel ashamed, since you have just told me, after an absence of three
years, that I look six years older. And still I have not learned to

smoke, even as I have not learned to play the flute – the flute I always like to hear sobbing beyond the courtyard in the night. Sometimes near, sometimes far away, it makes me think of the height of mountains.

It is like the sound of a flute, this light and languishing smoke which floats before us.

Please smoke, take one more.

I do not care for coffee but I'll sip green tea with pleasure.

Through the window the setting sun glows on the smoke
and tints it with dream-colour.

Don't you wish we were children again, sitting on a door-step, watching a white heron plunge into the rosy cloud beyond the river?

Please smoke, take another.

And thank you for bringing me a whiff of smoke from my native South.

CECIL DAY LEWIS
(b. 1904)

I

The Storm Rises

(*Georgics*, Book I, lines 351–392)

So that we might be able to predict from manifest signs
These things – heatwaves and rain and winds that bring cold
    weather,
The Father himself laid down what the moon's phases should
    mean,
The cue for the south wind's dropping, the sign that often noted
Should warn a farmer to keep his cattle nearer the shippon.
At once, when winds are rising,
The sea begins to fret and heave, and a harsh crackling
Is heard from timbered heights, or a noise that carries far
Comes confused from the beaches, and copses moan crescendo.
At such a time are the waves in no temper to bear your curved
    ship –
A time when gulls are blown back off the deepsea flying
Swift and screeching inland, a time when cormorants
Play on dry land, and the heron
Leaves his haunt in the fens to flap high over the cloud.
Another gale-warning often is given by shooting stars
That streak downsky and blaze a trail through the night's
    blackness
Leaving a long white wake:
Often light chaff and fallen leaves eddy in the air,
Or feathers play tig skimming along the skin of water.
But when lightning appears from the quarter of the grim north
    wind,
When it thunders to south or west, then all the countryside
Is a-swim with flooded dykes and all the sailors at sea

Close-reef their dripping sails. No, rain need never take us
Unawares: for high-flying cranes will have flown to valley
    bottoms
To escape the rain as it rises, or else a calf has looked up
At the sky and snuffed the wind with nostrils apprehensive.
Or the tittering swallow has flitted around and around the lake,
And frogs in the mud have croaked away at their old complaint.
Often too from her underground workings the emmet, wearing
A narrow path, bears out her eggs; a giant rainbow
Bends down to drink; rook armies desert their feeding-ground
In a long column, wing-tip to wing-tip, their wings whirring.
Now seabirds after their kind, and birds that about Caÿster's
Asian waterflats grub in the fresh pools, zestfully fling
Showers of spray over their shoulders,
Now ducking their heads in the creeks, scampering now at the
    wavelets,
Making a bustle and frivolous pantomime of washing.
Then the truculent raven full-throated announces rain
As she stalks alone on the dry sand.
Even at night can girls, spinning their wool, be aware
That a storm approaches, for then they behold in the burning lamp
The oil sputter and crumbly mould collect on the wick.

2

The Sleep of Palinurus

(*Aeneid*, Book V, lines 835–871)

And now the dewy night had nearly come to its halfway
Mark in the heavens: the mariners, sprawled on the hard benches
Beside their oars, were all relaxed in solacing quiet.
Just then did Sleep come feathering down from the stars above,
Lightly displacing the shadowy air, parting the darkness,
In search of you, Palinurus, carrying death in a dream
To your staunch heart. Now, taking the shape of Phorbas, the
    Sleep-god
Perched up there in the stern-sheets and rapidly spoke these
    words –

Palinurus, son of Iasus, the seas are bearing the ships on,
Steadily blows the breeze, and you have a chance to rest.
Lay your head down, and take a nap; your eyes are tired with
Watching. I will stand your trick at the helm for a little.
  Palinurus could hardly raise his heavy eyes, but he answered –
  Are you asking me to forget what lies behind the pacific
Face of the sea and its sleeping waves? to trust this devil?
What? Shall I leave Aeneas to the mercy of tricky winds –
I who, time and again, have been taken in by a clear sky?
  While he spoke, Palinurus kept a good grip on the tiller –
By no means would he release it – and a steadfast gaze on the stars.
But look! over his temples the god is shaking a bough
That drips with the dew of Lethe, the drowsy spell of Stygian
Waters. And now, though he struggles, his swimming eyes are
      closing.
As soon as, taken off guard, he was relaxed in unconsciousness,
The god, leaning down over him, hurled him into the sea
Still gripping the tiller; a part of the taffrail was torn away:
As he fell, he kept calling out to his friends, but they did not hear
      him.
Up and away skywards the Sleep-god now went winging.
Safe as before, the fleet was scudding upon its course –
Nothing to fear, for Neptune had guaranteed a safe passage.
And now, racing on, they were near the rocky place of the Sirens,
Dangerous once for mariners, white with the bones of many;
From afar the rasp of the ceaseless surf on those rocks could be
      heard.
Just then Aeneas became aware that his ship was yawing
Badly, her helmsman missing; he brought her back on to course
In the night sea, and deeply sighing, stunned by the loss of his
      friend, said –
  O Palinurus, too easily trusting clear sky and calm sea,
You will lie on a foreign strand, mere jetsam, none to bury you.

THEODOOR WEEVERS
(b. 1904)

FROM THE DUTCH OF ALBERT VERWEY

The Terraces at Meudon

The air is still: on hills in endless distance
Stretches the town in blond and rosy haze –
I turn to where soft laughter sounds and whispers:
A youth has kissed a sweetly radiant face.

I look below: stern lies there, firmly bounded,
Sombre around a pond an autumn park.
I look on high: a dome, of greystone rounded,
Towers over trees, – built to observe the stars.

On terrace-steps, now crumbling, but enduring,
Pausing in thoughtful wistfulness I stay, –
For lifeless things yet are the longer-during
Than we who, growing, wilting, pass away.

NORMAN CAMERON

(1905–1953)

I

The Lament of the fair Heaulmière

Methinks I hear the harlot wail
Who was the helmet-maker's lass,
Wishing herself still young and hale,
And crying in her woe: 'Alas!
Old Age, so cruel and so crass,
Why hast thou struck me down so soon?
What holds me back that, in this pass,
I do not seek death's final boon?

'Hast robb'd me of that mighty sway
Which beauty gave me at my birth
O'er all men, clerical or lay.
Once there was not a man on earth
But would have given all his worth,
Could he but win of me that prize
Which now, in these my days of dearth,
Even the beggars do despise.

'There's many a man I could have had,
But flouted, in my foolishess,
For love of a sharp-witted lad
On whom I shower'd my largesse.
Others might buy a feign'd caress:
'Twas he I lov'd, more than myself,
Whom he did cruelly oppress,
And lov'd me only for my pelf.

'And yet his bitterest attack
Could never cause my love to die.
He could have dragg'd me on my back

Or trampled me – did he but cry
"Kiss me!" away my woes would fly.
That beast, that slimy manikin,
Would cuddle me . . . And what have I
Left for it all? Disgrace and sin!

'Well, thirty years ago he died,
And I am left here, old and hoar.
When I bethink my days of pride,
What I am now, and was of yore,
Or when I hold a glass before
My naked body, now so chang'd,
Wrinkled and shrunken, frail and poor,
My wits with grief are nigh estrang'd.

'Where is that forehead's fair expanse;
That golden hair; those arching brows;
Those wide-set eyes; that pretty glance,
With which I charm'd the most morose;
Those little ears; that dainty nose,
Neither too tiny nor too great;
That dimpled chin; those Cupid's bows
Of lips; those teeth so white and straight?

'Where are the shoulders neat and slender;
Those long, soft arms; those fingers brent;
Those little breasts; those haunches tender,
High-rais'd and smooth and plainly meant
For riders in love's tournament;
Those ample loins, firm thighs, and twat
Set like a graceful monument
Within its handsome garden-plot?'

The forehead scowls, the hair is grey,
The brows are gone, the eyes are blear
That were so mocking and so gay
They fill'd the passer-by with cheer;
The nose is hook'd and far from fair,
The ears are rough and pendulous,
The face is sallow, dead and drear,
The chin is purs'd, the lips hang loose.

Aye, such is human beauty's lot!
The arms are short; the hands clench tight;
The shoulders tangle in a knot;
The breasts, in shame they shrink from sight;
Nipple and haunch, they share their plight;
The twat – ah, bah! The thighs are thin
As wither'd hams, and have a blight
Of freckles, like a sausage-skin.

''Tis thus we mourn for good old days,
Perch'd on our buttocks, wretched crones,
Huddled together by the blaze
Of some poor fire of forest cones,
That dies as quickly as our moans,
A briefly-lit, brief-living flame –
We who have sat on lovers' thrones! . . .
With many a man 'tis just the same.'

2

From the Ballad of Fat Margie

If I do serve my love with all my heart,
Must you, then, take me for a rogue or sot?
For certain charms she hath no counterpart.
With her I am a very Lancelot:
When people come, I run to drink a pot,
I 'go for wine' with soft and nimble tread,
I fetch them water, cheese and fruit and bread,
If they pay well, I cry them: '*Bene stat*;
Pray come again, when you've a load to shed,
To this bordèl where we are thron'd in state!'
But afterwards a bitter brawl may start,
When Margie comes back home without a groat.
Then hatred of her stabs me like a dart;
I seize her gown, her girdle and her coat
And swear I'll sell them all to pay her scot;
Whereat she screams, with arms akimbo spread,
And swears, by all the living and the dead,

It shall not be! And then I seize a slat
And score her face with notches fiery red,
In this bordèl where we are thron'd in state.

Then peace is made and she lets flee a fart,
Like an envenom'd beetle all a-bloat,
And lays her hand upon my privy part.
'Go, go!' she cries, and smites my tender spot.
Both drunk, we slumber like a worn-out boot.
At dawn her rumbling stomach wakes her greed;
She mounts me, eager not to waste my seed.
I groan beneath her, flatten'd by her weight,
Until the very life of me is sped,
In this bordèl where we are thron'd in state.

Come wind, come hail, come frost, I've bak'd my bread.
A lecher to a lecheress is wed.
Which is the worse? There's little to be said.
Like unto like: 'Bad cat for a bad rat.'
We love the mire, and miry is our bed;
We flee from honour, honour now is fled,
In this bordèl where we are thron'd in state.

FROM THE FRENCH OF ARTHUR RIMBAUD

Poor People in Church

Between oak benches, in mean corners stowed away,
Warming the air with fetid breath, fixing their vision
On the gilt-dripping chancel's twenty mouths, which bray
The pious canticles with meaningless precision;

Sniffing the wax like fragrant bread, and revelling,
Like dogs that have been whipped, in their humiliation,
The Poor unto dear God, the master and the king,
Offer their laughable and stubborn supplication.

The women are well pleased to wear the benches smooth
After the six black days that God has just bestowed!
Tangled in curious swaddling-clothes, they rock and soothe
Their hardly-human babes, a weeping, fatal load.

Their grimy bosoms bared, these feeders upon soup,
With a prayer in their eyes, though they have never prayed,
Are watching the unseemly movements of a group
Of pert young girls, who in their battered hats parade.

Outside are cold and hunger, husbands on the booze.
Well, there's this hour; then come the evils without names.
Meanwhile, all round them, whining, snuffling, whispering news,
Sits a whole gathering of ancient, dewlapped dames.

The timid ones, the epileptic ones, from whom
Yesterday at the cross-roads people turned aside,
The blind ones, nosing at old missels in the gloom,
Who creep into the court-yards with a dog for guide;

All, slavering their stupid beggars' creed, recite
Their endless plaint to Jesus, while he dreams on high
Beyond the murky window, in its yellowed light,
Far from thin evil ones, far from the fat and sly,

Far from the smells of meat, the smells of musty serge,
Prostrate and sombre farce in loathsome pantomime.
And now the worship blossoms with a keener urge,
The mysticalities become still more sublime,

When, coming from the naves through which no sunlight files,
Banal in silk, the Ladies of the town's best quarter
– O Christ! – the ones with liver-trouble and green smiles,
Offer bleached fingers to the kiss of holy-water.

STANLEY KUNITZ
(b. 1905)

FROM THE RUSSIAN OF ANDREI VOZNESENSKY

Fire in the Architectural Institute

Fire in the Architectural Institute!
through all the rooms and over the blueprints
like an amnesty through the jails . . .
Fire! Fire!

High on the sleepy façade
shamelessly, mischievously
like a red-assed baboon
a window skitters.

We'd already written our theses,
the time had come for us to defend them.
They're crackling away in a sealed cupboard:
all those bad reports on me!

The drafting paper is wounded,
it's a red fall of leaves;
my drawing-boards are burning,
whole cities are burning,

Five summers and five winters shoot up in flames
like a jar of kerosene.
Karen, my pet,
Oi! we're on fire!

Farewell architecture:
it's down to a cinder
for all those cowsheds decorated with cupids
and those post-offices in rococo!

O youth, phoenix, ninny,
your dissertation is hot stuff,
flirting its little red skirt now,
flaunting its little red tongue.

Farewell life in the sticks!
Life is a series of burned-out sites.
Nobody escapes the bonfire:
if you live – you burn.

But tomorrow, out of these ashes,
more poisonous than a bee
your compass-point will dart
to sting you in the finger.

Everything's gone up in smoke,
and there's no end of people sighing.
It's the end?
         It's only the beginning.
Let's go to the movies!

KENNETH REXROTH
(b. 1905)

FROM THE LATIN

From Carmina Burana

I am constantly wounded
By the deadly gossip that adds
Insult to injury, that
Punishes me mercilessly
With the news of your latest
Scandal in my ears. Wherever
I go the smirking fame of each
Fresh despicable infamy
Has run on ahead of me.
Can't you learn to be cautious
About your lecheries?
Hide your practices in darkness;
Keep away from raised eyebrows.
If you must murder love, do it
Covertly, with your candied
Prurience and murmured lewdness.

You were never the heroine
Of dirty stories in the days
When love bound us together.
Now those links are broken, desire
Is frozen, and you are free
To indulge every morbid lust,
And filthy jokes about your
Latest amour are the delight
Of every cocktail party.
Your boudoir is a brothel;
Your salon is a saloon;
Even your sensibilities
And your depraved innocence
Are only special premiums,
Rewards of a shameful commerce.

O the heart breaking memory
Of days like flowers, and your
Eyes that shone like Venus the star
In our brief nights, and the soft bird
Flight of your love about me;
And now your eyes are as bitter
As a rattlesnake's dead eyes,
And your disdain as malignant.
Those who give off the smell of coin
You warm in bed; I who have
Love to bring am not even
Allowed to speak to you now.
You receive charlatans and fools;
I have only the swindling
Memory of poisoned honey.

FROM THE GREEK OF ANTIPATROS

'Never again, Orpheus'

Never again, Orpheus
Will you lead the enchanted oaks,
Nor the rocks, nor the beasts
That are their own masters.
Never again will you sing to sleep
The roaring wind, nor the hail,
Nor the drifting snow, nor the boom
Of the sea wave.
You are dead now.
Led by your mother, Calliope,
The Muses shed many tears
Over you for a long time.
What good does it do us to mourn
For our sons when the immortal
Gods are powerless to save
Their own children from death?

FROM THE GREEK OF ASKLEPIADES

'Didyme waved her wand at me'

Didyme waved her wand at me.
I am utterly enchanted.
The sight of her beauty makes me
Melt like wax before the fire. What
Is the difference if she is black?
So is coal, but alight, it shines like roses.

FROM THE GREEK OF LEONIDAS

'Traveler in the wilds . . .'

Traveler in the wilds, do not
Drink this roiled, muddy, warm water,
But go on over the hill where
The cows are grazing, and by the
Shepherds' pine you will find a
Murmuring spring, flowing from the
Rock, cold as snow on the North Wind.

FROM THE
GREEK OF SULPUCIUS LUPERCUS SERVASIUS, JR

'Rivers level granite mountains'

Rivers level granite mountains,
Rains wash the figures from the sundial,
The plowshare wears thin in the furrow;
And on the fingers of the mighty,
The gold of authority is bright
With the glitter of attrition.

SAMUEL BECKETT
(b. 1906)

FROM THE FRENCH OF PAUL ELUARD

I

Scarcely Disfigured

Farewell sadness
Greeting sadness
Thou art inscribed in the lines of the ceiling
Thou art inscribed in the eyes that I love
Thou art not altogether want
For the poorest lips denounce thee
Smiling
Greeting sadness
Love of the bodies that are lovable
Mightiness of love that lovable
Starts up as a bodiless beast
Head of hope defeated
Sadness countenance of beauty.

2

Out of Sight in the Direction of My Body

All the trees all their boughs all their leaves
The grass at the base the rocks the massed houses
Afar the sea that thine eye washes
Those images of one day and the next
The vices the virtues that are so imperfect
The transparence of men in a fume from thy dour questing
Thy fixed ideas virgin-lipped leaden-hearted
The vices the virtues that are so imperfect
The eyes consenting resembling the eyes thou didst vanquish
The confusion of the bodies the lassitudes the ardours
The imitation of the words the attitudes the ideas.
The vices the virtues that are so imperfect

Love, is man unfinished.

WILLIAM EMPSON
(b. 1906)

FROM THE CHINESE

A Peasant Song

Now he has seen the girl Hsiang-Hsiang;
    Now back to the guerilla band.
And she goes with him down the vale,
    And pauses at the strand.

The mud is yellow, broad, and thick,
    And their feet stick, where the stream turns.
'Make me two models out of this,
    That clutches as it yearns.

'Make one of me and one of you,
    And both shall be alive.
Were there no magic in the dolls
    The children would not thrive.

'When you made them smash them back;
    They yet can live again.
Again make dolls of you and me,
    But mix them grain by grain.

'So your flesh will be part of mine,
    And part of mine be yours.
Brother and sister we shall be,
    Whose unity endures.

'Always the sister doll will cry,
    Made in these careful ways,
Cry on and on, Come back to me,
    Come back, in a few days.'

RICHMOND LATTIMORE
(b. 1906)

FROM THE GREEK OF ARCHILOCUS

The Wreckers and a former Friend

. . .

slammed by the surf on the beach
naked at Salmydéssos, where the screw-haired men
of Thrace, taking him in
will entertain him (he will have much to undergo,
chewing on slavery's bread)
stiffened with cold, and loops of seaweed from the slime
tangling his body about,
teeth chattering as he lies in abject helplessness
flat on his face like a dog
beside the beach break where the waves come shattering in.
And let me be there to watch;
for he did me wrong and set his heel on our good faith,
he who had once been my friend.

FROM THE GREEK OF THEOGNIS

'See, I have given you wings . . .'

See, I have given you wings on which to hover uplifted
   high above earth entire and the great waste of the sea
without strain. Wherever men meet in festivals, as men
   gather, you will be there, your name will be spoken again
as the young singers, with the flutes clear piping beside them,
   make you into a part of the winsome verses, and sing
of you. And even after you pass to the gloom and the secret
   chambers of sorrow, Death's house hidden under the ground,
even in death your memory shall not pass, and it shall not
   die, but always, a name and a song in the minds of men,

Kyrnos, you shall outrange the land of Greece and the islands,
  cross the upheaving sea where the fish swarm, carried not
astride the back of a horse, but the shining gifts of the dark-
      wreathed
  Muses shall be the force that carries you on your way.
For all wherever song is you shall be there for the singers.
  So long as earth endures and sun endures, you shall be.
I did this. But you give me not the smallest attention.
  You put me off with deceits as if I were a little child.

FROM THE GREEK OF IBYCUS

'In spring time the Kydonian quinces . . .'

In spring time the Kydonian
quinces, watered by running streams,
there where the maiden nymphs have
their secret garden, and grapes that grow
round in shade of the tendriled vine,
ripen.
          Now in this season for me
there is no rest from love.
Out of the hard bright sky,
a Thracian north wind blowing
with searing rages and hurt – dark,
pitiless, sent by Aphrodite – Love
rocks and tosses my heart.

FROM THE GREEK OF SAPPHO

I

'Some there are who say . . .'

Some there are who say that the fairest thing seen
on the black earth is an array of horsemen;
some, men marching; some would say ships; but I say
    she whom one loves best

is the loveliest. Light were the work to make this
plain to all, since she, who surpassed in beauty

all mortality, Helen, once forsaking
    her lordly husband,

fled away to Troy-land across the water.
Not the thought of child nor beloved parents
was remembered, after the Queen of Cyprus
    won her at first sight.

Since young brides have hearts that can be persuaded
easily, light things, palpitant to passion
as am I, remembering Anaktória
    who has gone from me

and whose lovely walk and the shining pallor
of her face I would rather see before my
eyes than Lydia's chariots in all their glory
    armored for battle.

2

To a Rival

You will die and be still, never shall be memory left of you
after this, nor regret when you are gone. You have not touched
    the flowers
of the Muses, and thus, shadowy still in the domain of Death,
you must drift with a ghost's fluttering wings, one of the darkened
    dead.

3

'When we lived all as one . . .'

When we lived all as one, she adored you as
symbol of some divinity,
Arignóta, delighted in your dancing.

Now she shines among Lydian women as
into dark when the sun has set
the moon, pale-handed, at last appeareth

making dim all the rest of the stars, and light
spreads afar on the deep, salt sea,
spreading likewise across the flowering cornfields;

and the dew rinses glittering from the sky;
roses spread, and the delicate
antherisk, and the lotus spreads her petals.

So she goes to and fro there, remembering
Atthis and her compassion, sick
the tender mind, and the heart with grief is eaten.

FROM THE GREEK OF AESCHYLUS

The Agamemnon Chorus

(lines 975–1033)

*[Agamemnon and Clytaemnestra enter the house. Cassandra
remains in the chariot. The Chorus speaks.]*

Why must this persistent fear
beat its wings so ceaselessly
and so close against my mantic heart?
Why this strain unwanted, unrepaid, thus prophetic?
Nor can valor of good hope
seated near the chambered depth
of the spirit cast it out
as dreams of dark fancy; and yet time
has buried in the mounding sand
the sea cables since that day
when against Ilium
the army and the ships put to sea.

Yet I have seen with these eyes
Agamemnon home again.
Still the spirit sings, drawing deep
from within this unlyric threnody of the Fury.
Hope is gone utterly,
the sweet strength is far away.
Surely this is not fantasy.

Surely it is real, this whirl of drifts
that spin the stricken heart.
Still I pray; may all this
expectation fade as vanity
into unfulfilment, and not be.

Yet it is true: the high strength of men
knows no content with limitation. Sickness
chambered beside it beats at the wall between.
Man's fate that sets a true
course yet may strike upon
the blind and sudden reefs of disaster.
But if before such time, fear
throw overboard some precious thing
of the cargo, with deliberate cast,
not all the house, laboring
with weight of ruin, shall go down,
nor sink the hull deep within the sea.
And great and affluent the gift of Zeus
in yield of ploughed acres year on year
makes void again sick starvation.

But when the black and mortal blood of man
has fallen to the ground before his feet, who then
can sing spells to call it back again?
Did Zeus not warn us once
when he struck to impotence
that one who could in truth charm back the dead men?
Had the gods not so ordained
that fate should stand against fate
to check any man's excess,
my heart now would have outrun speech
to break forth the water of its grief.
But this is so; I murmur deep in darkness
sore at heart; my hope is gone now
ever again to unwind some crucial good
from the flames about my heart.

FROM THE GREEK OF EURIPIDES

The Helen: Chorus

(lines 1106–1163)

CHORUS. To you, who deep forested, choired in the growth
of singing wood hide nested,
to you I utter my outcry,
to you, beyond all other birds sweet in your singing,
O nightingale of the sorrows
come, with brown beak shaken,
to the beat of your melody, come
with song to my sad singing
as I mourn for the hard sorrows
of Helen, for all the suffering,
all the tears of the daughters of Troy
from spears held by Achaeans,
all from the time when with outland oar he swept over
the water-flats, came, came, and his coming was sorrow
in marriage for Priam's people, moving
from Lacedaemon, from you, Helen: Paris, dark lover
brought there by Aphrodite.

And there were many Achaeans who by the spear
and by the stone's smash have died
and are given, in vain, to Hades.
For these, unhappy wives have cut their long hair.
The chambers of their love are left forsaken.
Many Achaeans besides
the man of the single oar drowned
off waterswept Euboea
when he lit his wreck fires, blazed
the false flares, and crashed them to death
on Aegean rocks at Caphereus.
And the harborless mountains of Malea in the storm wind
were death, when he fled from our land, with the prize of his
    outland
glory; prize, no prize, but war,
the Greek cloud shape his ship carried off,
the divine image of Hera.

What is god, what is not god, what is between man
and god, who shall say? Say he has found
the remote way to the absolute,
that he has seen god, and come
back to us, and returned there, and come
back again, reason's feet leaping
the void? Who can hope for such fortune?
Yourself were born. Helen, daughter to Zeus.
Winged in the curves of Leda there
as bird he childed you.
Yet even you were hallooed through Greece
as traitress, faithless, rightless, godless. No man's
thought I can speak of is ever clear.
The word of god only I found unbroken.

[Helen returns and joins Menelaus.]

Mindless, all of you, who in the strength of spears
and the tearing edge win your valors
by war, thus stupidly trying
to halt the grief of the world.
For if bloody debate shall settle
the issue, never again
shall hate be gone out of the cities of men.
By hate they won the chambers of Priam's city;
they could have solved by reason and words
the quarrel, Helen, for you.
Now these are given to the Death God below.
On the walls the flame, as of Zeus, lightened and fell.
And you, Helen, on your sorrows bear
more hardships still, and more matter for grieving.

VERNON WATKINS
(b. 1906)

FROM THE GERMAN OF HEINRICH HEINE

Sea-Sickness

The grey afternoon clouds
Droop, descending upon the sea
Which rises darkly to meet them,
And between them races the ship.

Sea-sick I sit, still, at the mast
And make meditations about myself,
Very old, ashen-grey meditations,
Which already Father Lot made
When he had enjoyed too much bounty
And found himself so ill afterwards.
Then, now and again, I think of old stories,
How cross-carrying pilgrims of earlier time
Believing, kissed, on the storm-tossed voyage,
The Virgin's image, rich in comfort,
How knights brought low in this sea-emergency
Pressed the dear glove of their cherished lady
Against their lips and were likewise comforted –
I, however, sit and chew disagreeably
An old herring, the salty comforter
In cat-crises and dog's distemper.

Meanwhile the ship contends
With the wild, upheaving tide;
It lands back now like a rearing war-horse
On the stern, so that the rudder cracks,
Now plunges down again headlong,
Into the chasm of moaning water,
Then again, as if carelessly love-weary,
It hovers, thinking to rest
On the black bosom of the giant wave

Which mightily rages on,
And suddenly, a confused sea-cataract,
Crashes into white water-curls
And covers my self with foam.

This rolling and hovering and pitching
Is unendurable!
Vainly my eye peers out, seeking
The German coast. But ah! only water,
And once again water, stirred-up water!

As the traveller in Winter longs at evening
For a hot cup of tea inside him,
So my heart now longs for you,
My German Fatherland.
Though your precious earth may always be covered
With insanity, hussars, bad verses,
And tepidly thin little treatises;
Although your zebras may always
Feed on roses instead of thistles,
Though your aristocratic apes may always
Swagger in grand, idle clothes refinedly,
And think themselves better than all the other
Heavily plodding low-browed cattle;
Though your council of snails may always
Consider itself immortal
Because it crawls on so slowly,
And though it may daily collect its votes
On whether the cheese belongs to the maggots,
And deliberate a long time
On how to perfect Egyptian sheep
So that their wool would grow better
And the shepherd could shear them like others
Without distinction –
Though folly and injustice may always
Cover you whole, O Germany;
Nevertheless I long for you,
For you are at least firm land.

WYSTAN HUGH AUDEN
(b. 1907)

FROM THE RUSSIAN OF AKHMADULINA

Volcanoes

Extinct volcanoes are silent:
Ash chokes craters and vent.
There giants hide from the sun
After the evil they have done.

Realms ever denser and colder
Weigh on each brutal shoulder,
But the old wicked visions keep
Visiting them in their sleep.

They behold a city, sure
Here summer will endure,
Though columns carved from congealed
Lava frame garden and field.

It is long ago: in sunlit hours
Girls gather armfuls of flowers
And Bacchantes give a meaning sign
To men as they sip their wine.

A feast is in progress: louder
The diners grow, more heated and lewder . . .
O my Pompei in your cindery grave,
Child of a princess and a slave!

What future did you assume,
What were you thinking of and whom
When you leaned your elbow thus
Thoughtlessly on Vesuvius?

Were you carried away by his stories?
Did you gaze with astonished eyes?

Didn't you guess – were you *that* innocent? –
Passion can be violent?

And then, when that day ended,
Did he lay a knowing forehead
At your dead feet? Did he, didn't he,
Bellow: 'Forgive me!'?

LOUIS MacNEICE
(1907–1963)

FROM THE GREEK OF AESCHYLUS

The Prophecy of Cassandra

(Lines from the *Agamemnon*)

CASS. Oh misery, misery!
Again comes on me the terrible labour of true
Prophecy, dizzying prelude; distracts . . .
Do you see these who sit before the house,
Children, like the shapes of dreams?
Children who seem to have been killed by their kinsfolk,
Filling their hands with meat, flesh of themselves,
Guts and entrails, handfuls of lament –
Clear what they hold – the same their father tasted.
For this I declare someone is plotting vengeance –
A lion? Lion but coward, that lurks in bed,
Good watchdog truly against the lord's return –
My lord, for I must bear the yoke of serfdom.
Leader of the ships, overturner of Troy,
He does not know what plots the accursed hound
With the licking tongue and the pricked-up ear will plan
In the manner of a lurking doom, in an evil hour.
A daring criminal! Female murders male.
What monster could provide her with a title?
An amphisbaena or hag of the sea who dwells
In rocks to ruin sailors –
A raving mother of death who breathes against her folk
War to the finish. Listen to her shout of triumph,
Who shirks no horrors, like men in a rout of battle.
And yet she poses as glad at their return.
If you distrust my words, what does it matter?
That which will come will come. You too will soon stand here
And admit with pity that I spoke too truly.

LEADER. Thyestes' dinner of his children's meat
    I understood and shuddered, and fear grips me
    To hear the truth, not framed in parables.
    But hearing the rest I am thrown out of my course.

CASS. It is Agamemnon's death I tell you you shall witness.

LEADER. Stop! Provoke no evil. Quiet your mouth!

CASS. The god who gives me words is here no healer.

LEADER. Not if this shall be so. But may some chance avert it.

CASS. *You* are praying. But others are busy with murder.

GEORGE REAVEY
(b. 1907)

FROM THE RUSSIAN OF VLADIMIR MAYAKOVSKY

To his beloved Self, the Author dedicates these lines

Four words,
heavy as a blow:
'... unto Caesar ... unto god ...'
But where can a man
like me
bury his head?
Where is there shelter for me?

If I were
as small
as the Great Ocean,
I'd tiptoe on the waves
and woo the moon like the tide.
Where shall I find a beloved,
a beloved like me?
She would be too big for the tiny sky!

Oh, to be poor!
Like a multimillionaire!
What's money to the soul?
In it dwells an insatiable thief.
The gold of all the Californias
will never satisfy the rapacious horde of my lusts.

Oh, to be tongued-tied
like Dante
or Petrarch!
I'd kindle my soul for one love alone!
In verse I'd command her to burn to ash!
And if my words
and my love
were a triumphal arch,

then grandly
all the heroines of love through the ages
would pass through it, leaving no trace.

Oh, were I
as quiet
as thunder
then I would whine
and fold earth's aged hermitage in my shuddering embrace.

If,
to its full power,
I used my vast voice,
the comets would wring their burning hands
and plunge headlong in anguish.

With my eyes' rays I'd gnaw the night –
if I were, oh,
as dull
as the sun!
Why should I want
to feed with my radiance
the earth's lean lap!

I shall go by,
dragging my burden of love.
In what delirious
and ailing
night,
was I sired by Goliaths –
I, so large,
so unwanted?

STEPHEN SPENDER
(b. 1909)
(with J. L. Gili)

FROM THE SPANISH OF FEDERICO GARCIA LORCA

Lament for Ignacio Sanchez Mejias

'COGIDA' AND DEATH

At five in the afternoon.
It was exactly five in the afternoon.
A boy brought the white sheet
at five in the afternoon.
A frail of lime ready prepared
at five in the afternoon.
The rest was death, and death alone
at five in the afternoon.

The wind carried away the cottonwool
at five in the afternoon.
And the oxide scattered crystal and nickel
at five in the afternoon.

Now the dove and the leopard wrestle
at five in the afternoon.
And a thigh with a desolate horn
at five in the afternoon.
The bass-string struck up
at five in the afternoon.
Arsenic bells and smoke
at five in the afternoon.
Groups of silence in the corners
at five in the afternoon.
And the bull alone with a high heart!
At five in the afternoon,
When the sweat of snow was coming
at five in the afternoon,

when the bull-ring was covered in iodine
at five in the afternoon,
death laid eggs in the wound
at five in the afternoon.
At five in the afternoon.
Exactly at five o'clock in the afternoon.
A coffin on wheels is his bed
at five in the afternoon.
Bones and flutes resound in his ears
at five in the afternoon.
Now the bull was bellowing inside his forehead
at five in the afternoon.
The room was iridescent with agony
at five in the afternoon.
From far off the gangrene is now coming
at five in the afternoon.
Lily-trumpet around his green groins
at five in the afternoon.
His wounds were burning like suns
at five in the afternoon.
and the crowd was breaking the windows
at five in the afternoon.
At five in the afternoon.
Ah, that terrible five in the afternoon!
It was five by all the clocks!
It was five in the shade of the afternoon!

ROBERT FITZGERALD
(b. 1910)

FROM THE LATIN OF HORACE

'The young men come less often . . .'
(*Odes*, Book I, 25)

The young men come less often – isn't it so? –
To rap at midnight on your fastened window;
Much less often. How do you sleep these days?

There was a time your door gave with proficiency
On easy hinges; now it seems apter at being shut.
I do not think you hear many lovers moaning

'Lydia, how can you sleep?'
'Lydia, the night is so long!'
'Oh, Lydia, I'm dying for you!'

No. The time is coming when *you* will moan
And cry to scornful men from an alley corner
In the dark of the moon when the wind's in a passion

With lust that would drive a mare wild
Raging in your ulcerous old viscera.
You'll be alone and burning then

To think how happy boys take their delight
In fresh and tender buds, the blush of myrtle,
Consigning dry leaves to the winter sea.

FROM THE GREEK OF HOMER

I

The Nymph to Menelaus

Odyssey, Book IV

That fairest of unearthly nymphs replied:

'I'll tell you this, too, clearly as may be.
When the sun hangs at high noon in heaven,
the Ancient glides ashore under the Westwind,
hidden by shivering glooms on the clear water,
and rests in caverns hollowed by the sea.
There flippered seals, brine children, shining come
from silvery foam in crowds to lie around him,
exhaling rankness from the deep sea floor.
Tomorrow dawn I'll take you to those caves
and bed you down there. Choose three officers
for company — brave men they had better be —
the old ones has strange powers, I must tell you.
He goes amid the seals to check their number,
and when he sees them all, and counts them all,
he lies down like a shepherd with his flock.
Here is your opportunity: at this point
gather yourselves, with all your heart and strength,
and tackle him before he bursts away.
He'll make you fight — for he can take the forms
of all the beasts, and water, and blinding fire;
but you must hold on, even so, and crush him
until he breaks the silence. When he does,
he will be in that shape you saw asleep.
Relax your grip, then, set the Ancient free,
and put your questions, hero:
Who is the god so hostile to you,
and how will you go home on the fish-cold sea.'

2

Proteus Foretells

(*Odyssey*, Book IV)

        And this is all he answered:
'Laërtês' son, whose home is Ithaka.
I saw him weeping, weeping on an island.
The nymph Kalypso has him, in her hall.
No means of faring home are left him now;
no ship with oars, and no ship's company
to pull him on the broad back of the sea.
As to your own destiny, prince Meneláos,
you shall not die in the bluegrass land of Argos;
rather the gods intend you for Elysion
with golden Rhadamanthos at the world's end,
where all existence is a dream of ease.
Snowfall is never known there, neither long
frost of winter, nor torrential rain,
but only mild and lulling airs from Ocean
bearing refreshment for the souls of men —
the West Wind always blowing.

                           For the gods
hold you, as Helen's lord, a son of Zeus.'

3

Odysseus Battles the Waves

(*Odyssey*, Book V)

Two nights, two days, in the solid deep-sea swell
he drifted, many times awaiting death,
until with shining ringlets in the East
the dawn confirmed a third day, breaking clear
over a high and windless sea; and mounting
a rolling wave he caught a glimpse of land.
What a dear welcome thing life seems to children
whose father, in the extremity, recovers
after some weakening and malignant illness:

his pangs have gone, the gods have delivered him.
So dear and welcome to Odysseus
the sight of land, of woodland, on that morning.
It made him swim again, to get a foothold
on solid ground. But when he came in earshot
he heard the trampling roar of sea on rock,
where combers, rising shoreward, thudded down
on the sucking ebb – all sheeted with salt foam.
Here were no coves or harborage or shelter,
only steep headlands, rockfallen reefs and crags.
Odysseus' knees grew slack, his heart faint,
a heaviness came over him, and he said:
'A cruel turn, this. Never had I thought
to see this land, but Zeus has let me see it –
and let me, too, traverse the Western Ocean –
only to find no exit from these breakers.
Here are sharp rocks off shore, and the sea a smother
rushing around them; rock face rising sheer
from deep water; nowhere could I stand up
on my two feet and fight free of the welter.
No matter how I try it, the surf may throw me
against the cliffside; no good fighting there.
If I swim down the coast, outside the breakers,
I may find shelving shore and quiet water –
but what if another gale comes on to blow?
Then I go cursing out to sea once more.
Or then again, some shark of Amphitritè's
may hunt me, sent by the genius of the deep.
I know how he who makes earth tremble hates me.'

During this meditation a heavy surge
was taking him, in fact, straight on the rocks.
He had been flayed there, and his bones broken,
had not grey-eyed Athena instructed him:
he gripped a rock-ledge with both hands in passing
and held on, groaning, as the surge went by,
to keep clear of its breaking. Then the backwash
hit him, ripping him under and far out.
An octopus, when you drag one from his chamber,

comes up with suckers full of tiny stones:
Odysseus left the skin of his great hands
torn on that rock-ledge as the wave submerged him.
And now at last Odysseus would have perished,
battered inhumanly, but he had the gift
of self-possession from grey-eyed Athena.
So, when the backwash spewed him up again,
he swam out and along, and scanned the coast
for some landspit that made a breakwater.
Lo and behold, the mouth of a calm river
at length came into view, with level shores
unbroken, free from rock, shielded from wind –
by far the best place he had found.
But as he felt the current flowing seaward
he prayed in his heart:

                        'O hear me, lord of the stream:
how sorely I depend upon your mercy!
derelict as I am by the sea's anger.
Is he not sacred, even to the gods,
the wandering man who comes, as I have come,
in weariness before your knees, your waters?
Here is your servant; lord, have mercy on me.'
Now even as he prayed the tide at ebb
had turned, and the river god made quiet water,
drawing him in to safety in the shallows.
His knees buckled, his arms gave way beneath him,
all vital force now conquered by the sea.
Swollen from head to foot he was, and seawater
gushed from his mouth and nostrils. There he lay,
scarce drawing breath, unstirring, deathly spent.
In time, as air came back into his lungs
and warmth around his heart, he loosed the veil,
letting it drift away on the estuary
downstream to where a white wave took it under
and Ino's hands received it. Then the man
crawled to the river bank among the reeds
where, face down, he could kiss the soil of earth,
in his exhaustion murmuring to himself:

'What more can this hulk suffer? What comes now?
In vigil through the night here by the river
how can I not succumb, being weak and sick,
to the night's damp and hoarfrost of the morning?
The air comes cold from rivers before dawn.
But if I climb the slope and fall asleep
in the dark forest's undergrowth – supposing
cold and fatigue will go, and sweet sleep come –
I fear I make the wild beasts easy prey.'

But this seemed best to him, as he thought it over.
He made his way to a grove above the water
on open ground, and crept under twin bushes
grown from the same spot – olive and wild olive –
a thicket proof against the stinging wind
or Sun's blaze, fine soever the needling sunlight;
nor could a downpour wet it through, so dense
those plants were interwoven. Here Odysseus
tunnelled, and raked together with his hands
a wide bed – for a fall of leaves was there,
enough to save two men or maybe three
on a winter night, a night of bitter cold.
Odysseus' heart laughed when he saw his leaf-bed,
and down he lay, heaping more leaves above him.

A man in a distant field, no hearthfires near,
will hide a fresh brand in his bed of embers
to keep a spark alive for the next day;
so in the leaves Odysseus hid himself,
while over him Athena showered sleep
that his distress should end, and soon, soon.
In quiet sleep she sealed his cherished eyes.

4

Ajax Unforgiving

(*Odyssey*, Book XI)

Now other souls of mournful dead stood by,
each with his troubled questioning, but one

remained alone, apart: the son of Télamon,
Aîas, it was – the great shade burning still
because I had won favor on the beachhead
in rivalry over Akhilleus' arms.
The Lady Thetis, mother of Akhilleus,
laid out for us the dead man's battle gear,
and Trojan children, with Athena,
named the Danaan fittest to own them. Would
god I had not borne the palm that day!
For earth took Aîas then to hold forever,
the handsomest and, in all feats of war,
noblest of the Danaans after Akhilleus.
Gently therefore I called across to him:

'Aîas, dear son of royal Télamon,
you would not then forget, even in death,
your fury with me over those accurst
calamitous arms? – and so they were, a bane
sent by the gods upon the Argive host.
For when you died by your own hand we lost
a tower, formidable in war. All we Akhaians
mourn you forever, as we do Akhilleus;
and no one bears the blame but Zeus.
He fixed that doom for you because he frowned
on the whole expedition of our spearmen.
My lord, come nearer, listen to our story!
Conquer your indignation and your pride.'

But he gave no reply, and turned away,
following other ghosts toward Erebos.
Who knows if in that darkness he might still
have spoken, and I answered?

5

The Suitors Slain

(*Odyssey*, Book XXII)

Think of a catch that fishermen haul in to a halfmoon bay
in a fine-meshed net from the white-caps of the sea:

how all are poured out on the sand, in throes for the salt sea,
twitching their cold lives away in Hêlios' fiery air:
so lay the suitors heaped on one another.

6

Odysseus Speaks to Penelope of Death

(*Odyssey*, Book XXIII)

'My strange one,

must you again, and even now,
urge me to talk? Here is a plodding tale;
no charm in it, no relish in the telling.
Teirêsias told me I must take an oar
and trudge the mainland, going from town to town,
until I discover men who have never known
the salt blue sea, nor flavor of salt meat —
strangers to painted prows, to watercraft
and oars like wings, dipping across the water.
The moment of revelation he foretold
was this, for you may share the prophecy:
some traveller falling in with me will say:
"A winnowing fan, that on your shoulder, sir?"
There I must plant my oar, on the very spot,
with burnt offerings to Poseidon of the Waters:
a ram, a bull, a great buck boar. Thereafter
when I come home again, I am to slay
full hekatombs to the gods who own broad heaven,
one by one.

Then death will drift upon me
from seaward, mild as air, mild as your hand,
in my well-tended weariness of age,
contented folk around me on our island.
He said all this must come.'

JAMES VINCENT CUNNINGHAM
(b. 1911)

Epigram 1.33

In private she mourns not the late-lamented;
If someone's by her tears leap forth on call.
Sorrow, my dear, is not so easily rented.
They are true tears that without witness fall.

FROM THE LATIN OF STATIUS

Silvae 5, 4

What was my crime, youthful most gentle god,
What folly was it that I alone should lack,
Sweet Sleep, thy gifts? All herds, birds, beasts are still,
The curved mountains seem wearily asleep,
Streams rage with muted noise, the sea-wave falls,
And the still-nodding deep rests on the shore.
Seven times now returning Phoebe sees
My sick eyes stare, and so the morning star
And evening, so Tithonia glides by
My tears, sprinkling sad dew from her cool whip.
How, then, may I endure? Not though were mine
The thousand eyes wherewith good Argus kept
But shifting watch, nor all his flesh awake.
But now, alas! If this long night some lover
In his girl's arms should willingly repel thee,
Thence come sweet Sleep! Nor with all thy power
Pour through my eyes – so may they ask, the many,
More happy –; touch me with thy wand's last tip,
Enough, or lightly pass with hovering step.

FROM THE LATIN OF ST AMBROSE

Aeterne Rerum Conditor

Builder eternally of things,
Thou rulest over night and day,
Disposing time in separate times
That Thou mayst lessen weariness;

Now crows the herald of the day,
Watchful throughout the wasting dark,
To walkers in the night a clock
Marking the hours of dark and dawn.

The morning star arises now
To free the obscure firmament;
Now every gang and prowling doom
Forsakes the dark highways of harm.

The sailor now regathers strength,
The channels of the sea grow calm;
And now Peter, the living rock,
Washes his guilt in the last crow.

Then quickly let us rise and go;
The cock stirs up the sleepy-head,
And chides again the lie-a-bed;
The cock convicts them who deny.

And to cock-crow our hopes reply;
Thy grace refills our ailing hearts;
The sword of brigandage is hid;
And faith returns where faith had fled.

Jesu, look back on us who fall,
Straighten the conduct of our life;
If Thou lookst back, denials fail,
And guilt is melted in a tear.

Thou Light, illumine with Thy light
Our sleeping lethargy of soul;
Thy name the first our lips shall choose,
Discharging thus our vows to Thee.

CZESŁAW MIŁOSZ
(b. 1911)

FROM THE POLISH OF ANTONI SŁONIMSKI

To the Germans

Proudly looking at the ruins of the conquered city,
Carrying a short, bloody sword, from an empty yard
A Roman barbarian entered the house of Archimedes
When the legion of Marcellus conquered Syracuse.

Half-naked, breathing heavily, in his dusty helmet,
He stopped, his nostrils drinking in new blood and crime.
'Noli tangere circulos meos' –
Said Archimedes gently, drawing in the sand.

On the circle, along the diameter and the inscribed triangle
The blood ran in a dark and living sign.
Archimedes, defend yourself against the mercenary!
Archimedes, who are murdered today!

Your blood sank into the sand, but your spirit lives.
Not true. The spirit dies as well. Where do traces remain?
In the marble of your house are adders' nests.
The wind spins circles out of sand on ruined Hellas.

FROM THE POLISH OF CZESŁAW MIŁOSZ

A Poor Christian Looks at the Ghetto

Bees build around red liver,
Ants build around black bone.
It has begun: the tearing, the trampling on silks,
It has begun: the breaking of glass, wood, copper, nickel, silver,
    foam
Of gypsum, iron sheets, violin strings, trumpets, leaves, balls,
    crystals.
Poof! Phosphorescent fire from yellow walls
Engulfs animal and human hair.

Bees build around the honeycomb of lungs,
Ants build around white bone.
Torn is paper, rubber, linen, leather, flax,
Fiber, fabrics, cellulose, snakeskin, wire.
The roof and the wall collapse in flame and heat seizes the
    foundations.
Now there is only the earth, sandy, trodden down,
With one leafless tree.

Slowly, boring a tunnel, a guardian mole makes his way,
With a small red lamp fastened to his forehead.
He touches burned bodies, counts them, pushes on,
He distinguishes human ashes by their luminous vapor,
The ashes of each man by a different part of the spectrum.
Bees build around a red trace.
Ants build around the place left by my body.

I am afraid, so afraid of the guardian mole.
He has swollen eyelids, like a Patriarch
Who has sat much in the light of candles
Reading the great book of the species.
What will I tell him, I, a Jew of the New Testament,
Waiting two thousand years for the second coming of Jesus?
My broken body will deliver me to his sight
And he will count me among the helpers of death:
The uncircumcised.

FROM THE POLISH OF TYMOTEUSZ AKRPOWICZ

A Lesson of Silence

Whenever a butterfly
happened to fold
too violently its wings –
there was a call: silence, please!

As soon as one feather
of a startled bird
jostled against a ray –
there was a call: silence, please!

In that way were taught
how to walk without noise
the elephant on his drum,
man on his earth.

The trees were rising
mute above the fields
as rises the hair
of the horror-stricken.

FROM THE POLISH OF ZBIGNIEW HERBERT

I

Apollo and Marsyas

The real duel of Apollo
with Marsyas
(absolute ear
versus immense range)
takes place in the evening
when as we already know
the judges
have awarded victory to the god

bound tightly to a tree
meticulously stripped of his skin
Marsyas
howls
before the howl reaches his tall ears
he reposes in the shadow of that howl

shaken by a shudder of disgust
Apollo is cleaning his instrument

only seemingly
is the voice of Marsyas
monotonous
and composed of a single vowel
A a a

in reality
Marsyas relates
the inexhaustible wealth
of his body
bald mountains of liver
white ravines of food
rustling forests of lung
sweet hills of muscle
joints bile blood
the wintry wind of bone
trembles over the salt of memory
shaken by a shudder of disgust
Apollo is cleaning his instrument

now to the chorus
is joined the backbone of Marsyas
in principle the same A a a
only deeper with the addition of rust

this is already beyond the endurance
of the god with nerves of artificial fiber
along a gravel path
between box espaliers
the victor departs
wondering
whether out of Marsyas' howling
there will not some day arise
a new brand
of art — let us say — concrete

suddenly
at his feet
falls a petrified nightingale

he looks back
and sees
that the tree to which Marsyas was fastened
has gone white-haired

completely

2

Elegy of Fortinbras

Now that we're alone we can talk Prince man to man
though you lie on the stairs and see no more than a dead ant
nothing but black sun with broken rays
I could never think of your hands without smiling
and now when they lie on the stone like fallen nests
they are defenseless as before The end is exactly this
The hands lie apart The sword lies apart The head apart
and the knight's feet in soft slippers

You will have a soldier's funeral without having been a soldier
the only ritual I am acquainted with a little
There will be no candles no singing only cannon fuses and bursts
Crape dragged on the pavement helmets boots artillery horses
       drums drums I know nothing exquisite
those will be my maneuvers before I start to rule
one has to take the city by the neck and shake it a bit

Anyhow you had to perish Hamlet you were not for life
you believed in crystal notions not in human clay
Always in a spasm asleep you hunted chimeras
wolfishly you crunched the air only to vomit
you knew no human thing you did not know even how to breathe

Now you have peace Hamlet you accomplished what you had to
and you have peace The rest is not silence but belongs to me
you chose the easier part an elegant thrust
but what is heroic death compared with eternal watching
with a cold apple in one's hand on a narrow chair
with a view on the anthill and the clock's dial

Adieu Prince I have tasks a sewer project
and a decree on prostitutes and beggars
I must also elaborate a better system of prisons
since as you justly said Denmark is a prison
I go to my affairs This night was born
a star named Hamlet We shall never meet
what I will leave will not deserve tragedy

It is not for us to greet each other or bid farewell
           We live on archipelagoes
and that water these words what can they do What can they do
   Prince

FROM THE POLISH OF JERZY HARASYMOWICZ

A Green Lowland of Pianos

   in the evening
   as far as the eye can see
   herds
   of black pianos

   up to their knees
   in the mire
   they listen to the frogs

   they gurgle in water
   with chords of rapture

   they are entranced
   by froggish, moonish spontaneity

   after the vacation
   they cause scandals
   in a concert hall
   during the artistic milking
   suddenly they lie down
   like cows

   looking with indifference
   at the white flowers
   of the audience

   at the gesticulating
   of the ushers

GEORGE SUTHERLAND FRASER

(b. 1915)

FROM THE LATIN OF TIBULLUS

Book I, Elegy 5

How well I'd bear the break, my anger spoke it:
Nothing more distant than defiance now!
Now, with a quick and clever boy to whip me,
I'm whirling like a top across the flags!

Brand my wild heart, and hurt it, that hereafter
It love not bragging: tame my bristling words!
And yet be kind. How once we put together
Our heads, made furtive plots, were fond, recall!
Think, when you lay cast down by wretched sickness,
Who was it sprinkled cleansing sulphur round,
And who invoked, lest mournful dreams beset you,
Quiet sleep, thrice scattering the sacred meal?
Cowled, in loose tunic, through the small hours' silence,
Who at the crossroads made the ninefold vow?
This payment mine, another has the profit,
Lucky, who draws the interest on my prayers!
I feigned, poor frantic man (the gods unfriendly!)
I should be happy then, if you were safe.

'Life on the land! Let Delia watch my harvests,
While on the hot, hard floor they thresh the corn,
Or watch the clusters in the full vat heaping
When rapid feet tread out the shiny must;
And learn to count my flocks; and, as a loving
Mistress, to dandle talkative small slaves;
Learn to give grapes as offering for vintage,
Spiked ears in pledge for corn, brimmed bowls for flocks.
She'll manage every man and every matter
And leave no task for me in all my house.
Messalla visits us . . . the sweetest apples

Delia will pluck him from the choicest trees:
Such a great man, she'll be an anxious hostess,
Prepare and serve his meals, a waiting maid!'

Such were my dreams that now the crosswinds carry
To scatter in Armenia's scented vales!

Often with drink I seek to rout these sorrows,
But sorrow turns wine itself to tears,
Often with girls; but on joy's very margin
Love, that recalls my love, abandons me.
The one who leaves me then will talk of witchcraft,
And say – oh, shame! – you know unholy charms!
And yet it is not words that could bewitch me,
But looks, soft arms, and girlish golden hair:
Such to Haemonian Peleus once was Thetis,
The sea-blue Nereid on her bridled fish!
These charms could charm me!

                      Some rich lover wants you,
And his accomplice is some crafty bawd!
May blood defile her food, her mouth be bloody
As it gluts brewage mingled with much gall!
May ghosts around her ply, their plight bemoaning,
Yes, and the ghoul-bird skirl upon her roof!
Let her pluck grass from graveyards, dogged by hunger,
Seek pickings from the morsels left by wolves,
Howl through the streets with nothing round her middle,
Run at the crossways from wild yelping dogs!
So be it! A god confirms. Powers guard lovers.
Venus, renounced for no just cause, will rage.
So, Delia, leave this witch's griping lessons
In time, in time . . .

            In love must riches win?
For your poor man is your most trusty servant,
Your poor man soonest cleaves to your soft side,
Your poor man, in the crush, a sturdy comrade,
Pushes your hips and somehow makes a way,
Your poor man will draw off your muddy leggings
And loose the coverings from your snowy feet.

(I sing in vain! Fine words will not win open
That door, who knocks must have a plenteous hand!)

You, who carry the day, of my fate be wary!
Light Luck turns lightly on her turning wheel.
Not in vain now one waits at the threshold,
Patient, and looks about him, and withdraws,
And seems to pass the house, but soon returning
Will hawk himself at Delia's very doors!
Sly Love has a dodge afoot. Be gay, I beg you,
While you can: your sloop still bobs in a clear sea!

MARTIN S. ALLWOOD
(b. 1916)

FROM THE DANISH OF PIET HEIN

Noble Funerals Arranged

The Nobel prize
Needs a candidate
Of course, by the hopeful crowd
You're stunned,
But none are sufficiently
Well-known and great,
Or sufficiently
Moribund.
Remember, it's not
A scholarship late –
It is
A funeral benefit fund.

FROM THE DANISH OF TOVE DITLEVSEN

(with John Hollander and Inga Allwood)

The Eternal Three

There are two men in the world, who
Are crossing my path I see,
And one is the man I love,
The other's in love with me.

And one exists in the nightly dreams
Of my sombre soul evermore,
The other stands at the door of my heart
But I will not open the door.

And one once gave me a vernal breath
Of happiness squandered – alack!

The other gave me his whole, long life
And got never an hour back.

And one lives hot in the song of my blood
Where love is pure, unbound –
The other is one with the humdrum day
Where all our dreams are drowned.

Between these two every woman stands,
In love, belovèd, and white –
And once every hundred years it happens
That both in one unite.

DAVID EMERY GASCOYNE
(b. 1916)

FROM THE FRENCH OF PAUL ELUARD

Necessity

Without great ceremony on earth
Near those who keep their poise
On this misery of all repose
Right near the good way
In the dust of the serious
I establish relations between man and woman
Between the smeltings of the sun and the bag of bees
Between the enchanted grottoes and the avalanche
Between the care-rimmed eyes and the pealing laughter
Between the heraldic blackbird and the star of garlic
Between the leaden thread and the sound of the wind
Between the fountain of ants and the growing of strawberries
Between the horseshoe and the tips of the fingers
Between the chalcedony and winter in pins
Between the eye-ball tree and the recorded mimicry
Between the carotid and the ghost of salt
Between the auracaria and the head of a dwarf
Between the branching rails and the speckled dove
Between man and woman
Between my solitude and you.

JANEZ GRADISNIK

(b. 1917)

FROM THE SLOVENE OF CENE VIPOTNIK

A Visit

A Woman sits on my prison bed tonight,
ominously silent like the grass on graves,
her figure darker than the darkness,
her heavy shadow strays over me.

Where eyes should be two beetles,
two brilliant beetles sleep on the eyelids,
and often, as if their sleep were light,
they sprinkle iridescent silver from their wings.

Where heart should be, there a dark fist
opens its fingers in greedy ambush –
he who is faithful to life and light
will not easily escape its dreadful weight.

As if a roller squashed the heated limbs,
the walls pant wildly in compassion.
Oh, would their cry not die! Oh, would it reach
the space where people live, where forests burst into leaf!

Reverberating, distant, cherished stars
throw through the bars invulnerable wings,
the poisonous weariness that struck me down,
fades from my veins, my torpid sinews.

A wave of moonlight splashes
over the dark stature of my silent guest;
the night will pass, the tender throb of morning
promises the sun, the day that will endure.

ROBERT LOWELL
(b. 1917)

FROM THE FRENCH OF FRANÇOIS VILLON

Villon's Epitaph

Oh brothers, you live after us,
because we shared your revenue.
God may have mercy upon you,
if you have mercy upon us.
Five, six – you see us tied up here,
the flesh we overfed hangs here,
our carrion rots through skin and shirt,
and we, the bones, have changed to dirt.
Do not laugh at our misery:
pray God to save your souls and ours!

We hang in chains to satisfy
your justice and your violence,
brother humans – surely, you see
that all men cannot have good sense!
Here no man may look down on us –
Oh Child of Mary, pity us,
forgive our crimes – if dying well
saved even the poor thief from hell,
the blood of Christ will not run dry:
pray God to save your souls and ours!

The rain has soaked and washed us bare,
the sun has burned us black. Magpies
and crows have chiselled out our eyes,
have jerked away our beards and hair.
Our bodies have no time to rest:
our chains clank north, south, east and west,
now here, now there, to the wind's dance –
more beaks of birds than knives in France!
Do not join our fraternity:
pray God to save your souls and ours!

Prince Jesus, king of earth and air,
preserve our bodies from hell's powers –
we have no debts or business there.
We were not hanged to make you laugh.
Villon, who wrote our epitaph,
prays God to save your souls and ours!

FROM THE GERMAN OF HEINRICH HEINE

Heine Dying in Paris

I

DEATH AND MORPHINE

Yes, in the end they are much of a pair,
my twin gladiator beauties – thinner than a hair,
their bronze bell-heads hum with the void; one's more austere,
however, and much whiter; none dares cry down his character.
How confidingly the corrupt twin rocked me in his arms;
his poppy garland, nearing, hushed death's alarms
at sword-point for a moment.
Soon a pinpoint of infinite regression! And now that incident
is closed. There's no way out,
unless the other turn about
and, pale, distinguished, perfect, drop his torch.
He and I stand alerted for life's Doric, drilled, withdrawing march:
sleep is lovely, death is better still,
not to have been born is of course the miracle.

II

Every idle desire has died in my breast;
even hatred of evil things, even my feeling
for my own and other men's distress.
What lives in me is death.
The curtain falls, the play is done;
my dear German public is goosestepping home, yawning.
They are no fools, these good people:

they are slurping their dinners quite happily,
bear-hugging beer-mugs – singing and laughing.

That fellow in Homer's book was quite right:
he said: the meanest little Philistine living
in Stukkert-am-Neckar is luckier
than I, the golden-haired Achilles, the dead lion,
glorious shadow-king of the underworld.

III

My zenith was luckily happier than my night:
whenever I touched the lyre of inspiration, I smote
the Chosen People. Often – all sex and thunder –
I pierced those overblown and summer clouds . . .
But my summer has flowered. My sword is scabbarded
in the marrow of my spinal discs.
Soon I must lose all these half-gods
that made my world so agonizingly half-joyful.

FROM THE FRENCH OF CHARLES BAUDELAIRE

The Voyage

(*For T. S. Eliot*)

I

For the boy playing with his globe and stamps,
the world is equal to his appetite –
how grand the world in the blaze of the lamps,
how petty in tomorrow's small dry light!

One morning we lift anchor, full of brave
prejudices, prospects, ingenuity –
we swing with the velvet swell of the wave,
our infinite is rocked by the fixed sea.

Some wish to fly a cheapness they detest,
others, their cradles' terror – others stand
with their binoculars on a woman's breast,
reptilian Circe with her junk and wand.

Not to be turned to reptiles, such men daze
themselves with spaces, light, the burning sky;
cold toughens them, they bronze in the sun's blaze
and dry the sores of their debauchery.

But the true voyagers are those who move
simply to move – like lost balloons! Their heart
is some old motor thudding in one groove.
It says its single phrase, 'Let us depart!'

They are like conscripts lusting for the guns;
our sciences have never learned to tag
their projects and designs – enormous, vague
hopes grease the wheels of these automatons!

II

We imitate, oh horror! tops and bowls
in their eternal waltzing marathon;
even in sleep, our fever whips and rolls –
like a black angel flogging the brute sun.

Strange sport! where destination has no place
or name, and may be anywhere we choose –
where man, committed to his endless race,
runs like a madman diving for repose!

Our soul is a three-master seeking port:
a voice from starboard shouts, 'We're at the dock!'
Another, more elated, cries from port,
'Here's dancing, gin and girls!' Balls! it's a rock!

The islands sighted by the lookout seem
the El Dorados promised us last night;
imagination wakes from its drugged dream,
sees only ledges in the morning light.

What dragged these patients from their German spas?
Shall we throw them in chains, or in the sea?
Sailors discovering new Americas,
who drown in a mirage of agony!

The worn-out sponge, who scuffles through our slums
sees whiskey, paradise and liberty
wherever oil-lamps shine in furnished rooms –
we see Blue Grottoes, Caesar and Capri.

III

Stunningly simple Tourists, your pursuit
is written in the tear-drops in your eyes!
Spread out the packing cases of your loot,
your azure sapphires made of seas and skies!

We want to break the boredom of our jails
and cross the oceans without oars or steam –
give us visions to stretch our minds like sails,
the blue, exotic shoreline of your dream!

Tell us, what have you seen?

IV

                 'We've seen the stars,
a wave or two – we've also seen some sand;
although we peer through telescopes and spars,
we're often deadly bored as you on land.

'The shine of sunlight on the violet sea,
the roar of cities when the sun goes down:
these stir our hearts with restless energy;
we worship the Indian Ocean where we drown!

'No old chateau or shrine besieged by crowds
of crippled pilgrims sets our souls on fire,
as these chance countries gathered from the clouds.
Our hearts are always anxious with desire.

'Desire, that great elm fertilized by lust,
gives its old body, when the heaven warms
its bark that winters and old age encrust;
green branches draw the sun into its arms.

'Why are you always growing taller, Tree –
Oh longer-lived than cypress! Yet we took
one or two sketches for your picture-book,
Brothers who sell your souls for novelty!

'We have salaamed to pagan gods with horns,
entered shrines peopled by a galaxy
of Buddhas, Slavic saints, and unicorns,
so rich Rothschild must dream of bankruptcy!

'Priests' robes that scattered solid golden flakes,
dancers with tatooed bellies and behinds,
charmers supported by braziers of snakes . . .'

V

Yes, and what else?

VI

Oh trivial, childish minds!

You've missed the more important things that we
were forced to learn against our will. We've been
from top to bottom of the ladder, and see
only the pageant of immortal sin:

there women, servile, peacock-tailed, and coarse,
marry for money, and love without disgust
horny, pot-bellied tyrants stuffed on lust,
slaves' slaves – the sewer in which their gutter pours!

old maids who weep, playboys who live each hour,
state banquets loaded with hot sauces, blood and trash,
ministers sterilized by dreams of power,
workers who love their brutalizing lash;

and everywhere religions like our own
all storming heaven, propped by saints who reign
like sybarites on beds of nails and frown –
all searching for some orgiastic pain!

Many, self-drunk, are lying in the mud –
mad now, as they have always been, they roll
in torment screaming to the throne of God:
'My image and my lord, I hate your soul!'

And others, dedicated without hope,
flee the dull herd – each locked in his own world
hides in his ivory-tower of art and dope –
this is the daily news from the whole world!

VII

How sour the knowledge travellers bring away!
The world's monotonous and small; we see
ourselves today, tomorrow, yesterday,
an oasis of horror in sands of ennui!

Shall we move or rest? Rest, if you can rest;
move if you must. One runs, but others drop
and trick their vigilant antagonist.
Time is a runner who can never stop,

the Wandering Jew or Christ's Apostles. Yet
nothing's enough; no knife goes through the ribs
of this retarius throwing out his net;
others can kill and never leave their cribs.

And even when Time's heel is on our throat
we still can hope, still cry, 'On, on, let's go!'
Just as we once took passage on the boat
for China, shivering as we felt the blow,

so we now set our sails for the Dead Sea,
light-hearted as the youngest voyager.
If you look seaward, Traveller, you will see
a spectre rise and hear it sing, 'Stop, here,

and eat my lotus-flowers, here's where they're sold.
Here are the fabulous fruits; look, my boughs bend;
eat yourself sick on knowledge. Here we hold
time in our hands, it never has to end.'

We know the accents of this ghost by heart;
Our comrade spreads his arms across the seas;
'On, on, Orestes. Sail and feast your heart –
Here's Clytemnestra.' Once we kissed her knees.

VIII

It's time. Old Captain, Death, lift anchor, sink!
The land rots; we shall sail into the night;
if now the sky and sea are black as ink,
our hearts, as you must know, are filled with light.

Only when we drink poison are we well –
we want, this fire so burns our brain tissue,
to drown in the abyss – heaven or hell,
who cares? Through the unknown, we'll find the *new*.

FROM THE FRENCH OF ARTHUR RIMBAUD

The Sleeper in the Valley

The swollen river sang through the green hole,
and madly hooked white tatters on the grass.
Light escaladed the hot hills. The whole
valley bubbled with sunbeams like a beer-glass.

The conscript was open-mouthed; his bare head
and neck swam in the bluish water cress.
He slept. The mid-day soothed his heaviness,
sunlight was raining into his green bed,

and baked the bruises from his body, rolled
as a sick child might hug itself asleep . . .
Oh Nature, rock him warmly, he is cold.

The flowers no longer make his hot eyes weep.
The river sucks his hair. His blue eye rolls.
He sleeps. In his right side are two red holes.

FROM THE FRENCH OF PAUL VALÉRY

Helen

I am the blue! I come from the lower world
to hear the serene erosion of the surf;
once more I see the galleys bleed with dawn,
and shark with muffled rowlocks into Troy.
My solitary hands recall the kings;
I used to run my fingers through their beards;
I wept. They sang about their shady wars,
the great gulfs boiling sternward from their keels.
I hear the military trumpets, all that brass,
blasting commands to the frantic oars;
the rowers' metronome enchains the sea,
and high on beaked and dragon prows, the gods –
their fixed, archaic smiles stung by the salt –
reach out their carved, indulgent arms to me!

FROM THE ITALIAN OF EUGENIO MONTALE

The Chess Player

At last with stubborn jabs of your fingers
you kill the red cigarette bulb in the china dish;
expiring spirals of smoke
crinkle like lamb's fleece toward the ceiling,
and encumber the knights and bishops
on the chessboard, who hold their positions –
stupefied. Smoke-ring after smoke-ring snakes upward,
more agile than the gold mines on your fingers.

A window opens. One puff is enough
to panic the smoke's heaven-flung mirage
of imperial arches and battlements; –
down below another world moves:
a man, bruised by the sores of the wolf,
ignores your incense:
all the torture and formulae
of your small, heraldic, chessboard world.

For a time, I doubted if you yourself even
made any sense of the game, its square,
hobbled moves through gunpowder
clouds of tobacco . . . Poise cannot
pay off the folly of death; the flash
of your eyes asks that an answering crash
pierce the smoke-screen
thrown up by the god of chance to befriend you.

Today, I know what you want. I hear
the hoarse bell of the feudal campanile.
The archaic ivory chessmen are terrified.
Like snowmen, they melt in your mind's white glare.

FROM THE RUSSIAN OF BORIS PASTERNAK

I

In the Woods

A lilac heat sickened the meadow;
high in the wood, a cathedral's sharp, nicked groins.
No skeleton obstructed the bodies –
all was ours, obsequious wax in our fingers . . .

Such, the dream: you do not sleep,
you only dream you thirst for sleep,
that some one elsewhere thirsts for sleep –
two black suns singe his eyelashes.

Sunbeams shower and ebb to the flow of iridescent beetles.
The dragonfly's mica whirs on your cheek.
The wood fills with meticulous scintillations –
a dial under the clockmaker's tweezers.

It seemed we slept to the tick of figures;
in the acid, amber ether,
they set up nicely tested clocks,
shifted, regulated them to a soprano hair for the heat.

They shifted them here and there, and snipped at the wheels.
Day declined on the blue clock-face;

they scattered shadows, drilled a void –
the darkness was a mast derricked upright.

It seems a green and brown happiness flits beyond us;
sleep smothers the woods;
no elegiacs on the clock's ticking –
sleep, it seems, is all this couple is up to.

2

Hamlet in Russia, A Soliloquy

My heart throbbed like a boat on the water.
My oars rested. The willows swayed through the summer,
licking my shoulders, elbows and rowlocks –
wait! this might happen,

when the music brought me the beat,
and the ash-gray water-lilies dragged, and a couple of daisies
    blew,
and a hint of blue dotted a point off-shore –
lips to lips, stars to stars!

My sister, life!
the world has too many people for us,
the sycophant, the spineless –
politely, like snakes in the grass, they sting.

My sister!
embrace the sky and Hercules
who holds the world up forever
at ease, perhaps, and sleeps at night

thrilled by the nightingales crying . . .

The boat stops throbbing on the water . . .
The clapping stops. I walk into the lights
as Hamlet, lounge like a student against the door-frame,
and try to catch the far-off dissonance of life –
all that has happened, and must!

From the dark the audience leans its one hammering brow against
    me –
ten thousand opera glasses, each set on the tripod!
Abba, Father, all things are possible with thee –
take away this cup!

I love the mulishness of Providence,
I am content to play the one part I was born for . . .
quite another play is running now . . .
take me off the hooks tonight!

The sequence of scenes was well thought out;
the last bow is in the cards, or the stars –
but I am alone, and there is none . . .
All's drowned in the sperm and spittle of the Pharisee –

To live a life is not to cross a field.

JOHN HEATH-STUBBS
(b. 1918)

FROM THE ITALIAN OF GIACOMO LEOPARDI

To Himself

Now be for ever still,
Weary my heart. For the last cheat is dead,
I thought eternal. Dead. For us, I know
Not only the dear hope
Of being deluded gone, but the desire.
Rest still for ever. You
Have beaten long enough. And to no purpose
Were all your stirrings; earth not worth your sighs.
Boredom and bitterness
Is life; and the rest, nothing; the world is dirt.
Lie quiet now. Despair
For the last time. Fate granted to our kind
Only to die. And now you may despise
Yourself, nature, the brute
Power which, hidden, ordains the common doom,
And all the immeasurable emptiness of things.

EWALD OSERS
(b. 1917)

AND

J. K. MONTGOMERY
(b. 1873)

FROM THE CZECH OF F. SRAMEK

Spring 1923

The world is collapsing and crumbling
Behind a thin wall.
Blood-red are the crossbars of windows
As shades of night fall.
On torches the people are lying,
Sleep on them all.

Over the ridge is rising
A shadow of dread;
Hard is his chin and his mouth hard,
Helmet on head;
Under his cloak is a pitch-torch
Havoc to spread.

Now through the steppe and the forest
The shadow has passed.
Where is he marching, man's offspring,
Striding so fast?
He's gnawing his fingers and howling
Into the blast.

Let me take breath for a moment,
Pause ere I spring.
Under which flag shall I fight now?
Long live the king!
Of howling wolves and of she-wolves
The last to be king.

EWALD OSERS
(b. 1917)

Prague in the Mid-day Sun

It is late in the morning,
I am sitting under a coloured parasol – down there lies **Prague**;
After long rains an amethyst vapour is rising from her;
I see her through the filigree of trees as a maniac his phantasm;
I see her as a great ship whose mast is the Castle;
Like the enchanted cities of my visions,
Like the great ship of the Golden Corsair,
Like the dream of delirious architects,
Like the throned residence of Magic,
Like Saturn's palace with its gates flung open to the sun,
Like a volcano fortress hewn by a raving madman,
Like a guide to eremitic inspiration,
Like a volcano come to life again,
Like bracelets dancing in front of mirrors.

It is noon:
Prague is sleeping and yet awake, like a fantastic dragon,
Like a sacred rhinoceros whose cage is the sky,
Like a stalactite organ playing softly,
Like a symbol of resurrection and of treasures from dried-up lakes
Like an army in panoply saluting the emperor,
Like an army in panoply saluting the sun,
Like an army in panoply turned into jasper.

Enchanted city, far too long have I been gazing at you with blind
        eyes,
Looking for you in the distance, oh today I know it:
You are obscure as the fires deep in the rocks, as my fantasy,
Your beauty has sprung from caverns and subterranean agates,
You are old as the prairies over which song spreads its wings;
When your tower clocks strike you are opaque as an island night,

Exalted as the tombs, as the fillets of Ethiopian kings;
As if you were from a different world, a mirror of my imagery;
You are beautiful as the mystery of love and of improbable clouds,
You are beautiful as the mystery of speech and of primordial
    memory,
You are beautiful as an erratic block marked by the rains,
You are beautiful as the mystery of sleep, of stars and of
    phosphorescence,
You are beautiful as the mystery of thunder, of the magic lamp and
    of poetry.

TOM SCOTT
(b. 1918)

FROM THE FRENCH OF FRANÇOIS VILLON

I

Ballat o the Leddies o aulden times

Tell me whaur, in whit countrie
Bides Flora noo, yon Roman belle?
Whaur Archipiades, Thais be;
Thir douce cuisins, can ye tell
Whaur gossipin Echo draws pell-mell
Abuin some burn owre-hung wi bine
Her beautie's mair than human spell:
Aye, whaur are the snaws lang syne?

Whaur's Heloise, yon wyce abbess
Fur whome Pete Abelard manless fell,
Yet luvin still, at Saunt Denniss
Wroucht oot his days in cloistered cell?
And say whaur yon queen is as well
That ordert Buridan at dine
Be sacked an dumped in the Seine tae coo
Aye, whaur are the snaws lang syne?

Queen Blanche, as pure's the flooer-de-lys,
Whase voice nae siren's could excel,
Big-fuitit Bertha, Beatrice,
An her that ruled the Maine hersel,
Joan the Guid, the lass they tell
The English brunt, though near-divine ..
Whaur they are, Heiven's Queen, reveal:
Aye, whaur are the snaws lang syne?

Prince, this week I cannae well,
Nor this year, say whaur noo they shine.
Ask, ye'll but hear the owrecome swell:
Aye, whaur are the snaws lang syne?

TOM SCOTT

FROM THE ITALIAN OF DANTE

Paola and Francesca

Then I turnit back til them an said:
    Francesca, your disaster gars me greit
    Wi doole an pity. Tell me, whit was't made,
While still yir luve was biddable an sweet,
    (An bi whit snare yir weirdit sauls wer taen)
    Luve grant ye leave tae pree sic taintit meat?
And then she said: There is nae greater pain
    Than tae be mindet o lost happiness
    In misery, as your auld guide shud ken.
But if ye maun hear whye we dree aa this
    Fur luvin owre unwisely an owre-weill,
    I'll tell ye, though we doole, o oor first kiss.
Waan day we read thegither yon auld tale
    O' Launcelot, an hoo he pined in luve.
    We wer oorsels, an took nae thoucht o ill.
Mony a time oor gliffs exchanged abuve
    The page, an aa oor pallor turnit reid.
    But only waan thing could oor doonfaa pruve.
When, hoo that sair-saucht smile was kissed, we read,
    Bi sich a luver, he, I maun confess,
    Whom naethin noo will pairt me frae, though deid,
Fumblit on ma mooth a tremlin kiss.
    That buik, that author, Galeotto pruved.
    We read that day nae further on than this . . .
While the waan ghaist tellt me hoo they luved,
    The tither grat, till I could staun nae mair,
    An sank doun in a dwalm, I was sae muved,
Like a diein man, I sprachlet on the fluir.

FRAE THE GREEK O SAPPHO

Doun gaes the muin hersel, an aa
    The Pleiades forbye.
Nicht is nearin her mirkest hoor
    And yet alane I lie.

DENNIS JOSEPH ENRIGHT
(b. 1920)

FROM THE JAPANESE OF KŌTARŌ TAKAMURA

My Poetry

My poetry is not part of western poetry;
The two touch, circumference against circumference,
But never quite coincide ...
I have a passion for the world of western poetry,
But I do not deny that my poetry is formed differently.
The air of Athens and the subterranean fountain of Christianity
Have fostered the pattern of thought and diction of western
      poetry;
It strikes through to my heart with its infinite beauty and
      strength –
But its physiology, of wheat-meal and cheese and *entrecôtes*,
Runs counter to the necessities of my language.
My poetry derives from my bowels –
Born at the farthest limits of the far east,
Bred on rice and malt and soya-beans and the flesh of fish,
My soul – though permeated by the lingering fragrance of
      Gandhara
And later enlightened by the 'Yellow Earth' civilization of a vast
      continent
And immersed in the murmuring stream of the Japanese classics –
Now marvels excitedly at the power of the split atom ...
My poetry is no other than what I am,
And what I am is no other than a sculptor of the far east.
For me the universe is the prototype of composition,
And poetry is the composed counter-points.
Western poetry is my dear neighbour,
But the traffic of my poetry moves on a different path ...

RICHARD WILBUR

(b. 1921)

A Prayer to go to Paradise with the Donkeys

When I must come to you, O my God, I pray
It be some dusty-roaded holiday,
And even as in my travels here below,
I beg to choose by what road I shall go
To Paradise, where the clear stars shine by day.
I'll take my walking-stick and go my way,
And to my friends the donkeys I shall say,
'I am Francis Jammes, and I'm going to Paradise,
For there is no hell in the land of the loving God.'
And I'll say to them: 'Come, sweet friends of the blue skies,
Poor creatures who with a flap of the ears or a nod
Of the head shake off the buffets, the bees, the flies . . .'

Let me come with these donkeys, Lord, into your land,
These beasts who bow their heads so gently, and stand
With their small feet joined together in a fashion
Utterly gentle, asking your compassion.
I shall arrive, followed by their thousands of ears,
Followed by those with baskets at their flanks,
By those who lug the carts of mountebanks
Or loads of feather-dusters and kitchen-wares,
By those with humps of battered water-cans,
By bottle-shaped she-asses who halt and stumble,
By those tricked out in little pantaloons
To cover their wet, blue galls where flies assemble
In whirling swarms, making a drunken hum.
Dear God, let it be with these donkeys that I come,
And let it be that angels lead us in peace
To leafy streams where cherries tremble in air,
Sleek as the laughing flesh of girls; and there
In that haven of souls let it be that, leaning above

Your divine waters, I shall resemble these donkeys,
Whose humble and sweet poverty will appear
Clear in the clearness of your eternal love.

FROM THE FRENCH OF PAUL VALÉRY

Helen

It is I, O Azure, come from the caves below
To hear the waves clamber the loudening shores,
And see those barks again in the dawn's glow
Borne out of darkness, swept by golden oars.

My solitary hands call back the lords
Whose salty beards beguiled my finger-tips;
I wept. They sang the prowess of their swords
And what great bays fled sternward of their ships.

I hear the martial trumpets and the deep-
Sea conches cry a cadence to the sweeps;
The oarsmen's chantey holds the storm in sway;

And high on the hero prows the Gods I see,
Their antique smiles insulted by the spray,
Reaching their carved, indulgent arms to me.

FROM THE ITALIAN OF SALVATORE QUASIMODO

The Agrigentum Road

That wind's still there that I remember afire
In the manes of the racing horses
Veering across the plains; a wind
That stains the sandstone and erodes the hearts
Of downed columnar statues in the grass.
Oh antique soul, bled white
By rancor, back you lean to that wind again,
Catching the delicate fetor of the moss
That clothes those giants tumbled down by heaven.

How lonely it will be, the time that is left you!
    Worse, worse, if you should hear
That sound again, borne towards the far-off sea
Which Hesperus already pinks with morning:
The jew's-harp quavering sadly in the mouth
Of the wagon-maker climbing
Slowly his moon-washed hill, amidst
The murmur of the Saracen olive trees.

FROM THE FRENCH OF MOLIÈRE

Tartuffe

Act I, Scene 5

ORGON

Oh, had you seen Tartuffe as I first knew him,
Your heart, like mine, would have surrendered to him.
He used to come into our church each day
And humbly kneel nearby, and start to pray.
He'd draw the eyes of everybody there
By the deep fervour of his heartfelt prayer;
He'd sigh and weep, and sometimes with a sound
Of rapture he would bend and kiss the ground;
And when I rose to go, he'd run before
To offer me holy-water at the door.
His serving-man, no less devout than he,
Informed me of his master's poverty;
I gave him gifts, but in his humbleness
He'd beg me every time to give him less.
'Oh, that's too much,' he'd cry, 'too much by twice!
I don't deserve it. The half, Sir, would suffice.'
And when I wouldn't take it back, he'd share
Half of it with the poor, right then and there.
At length, Heaven prompted me to take him in
To dwell with us, and free our souls from sin.
He guides our lives, and to protect my honor
Stays by my wife, and keeps an eye upon her;

He tells me whom she sees, and all she does,
And seems more jealous than I ever was!
And how austere he is! Why, he can detect
A mortal sin where you would least suspect;
In smallest trifles, he's extremely strict.
Last week, his conscience was severely pricked
Because, while praying, he had caught a flea
And killed it, so he felt, too wrathfully.

Act III, Scene 3

TARTUFFE

I may be pious, but I'm human too:
With your celestial charms before his eyes,
A man has not the power to be wise.
I know such words sound strangely, coming from me,
But I'm no angel, nor was meant to be,
And if you blame my passion, you must needs
Reproach as well the charms on which it feeds.
Your loveliness I had no sooner seen
Than you became my soul's unrivalled queen;
Before your seraph glance, divinely sweet,
My heart's defenses crumbled in defeat,
And nothing fasting, prayer, or tears might do
Could stay my spirit from adoring you.
My eyes, my sighs have told you in the past
What now my lips make bold to say at last,
And if, in your great goodness, you will deign
To look upon your slave, and ease his pain, —
If, in compassion for my soul's distress,
You'll stoop to comfort my unworthiness,
I'll raise to you, in thanks for that sweet manna,
An endless hymn, an infinite hosanna.
With me, of course, there need be no anxiety,
No fear of scandal or of notoriety.
These young court gallants, whom all the ladies fancy,
Are vain in speech, in action rash and chancy;
When they succeed in love, the world soon knows it;
No favor's granted them but they disclose it

And by the looseness of their tongues profane
The very altar where their hearts have lain.
Men of my sort, however, love discreetly,
And one may trust our reticence completely.
My keen concern for my good name insures
The absolute security of yours;
In short, I offer you, my dear Elmire,
Love without scandal, pleasure without fear.

FROM THE RUSSIAN OF ANDREI VOZNESENSKY

Anti-Worlds

The clerk Bukashkin is our neighbour.
His face is grey as blotting-paper.

But like balloons of blue or red,
Bright Anti-Worlds
                float over his head!
On them reposes, prestidigitous,
Ruling the cosmos, a demon-magician,
Anti-Bukashkin the Academician,
Lapped in the arms of Lollobrigidas.

But Anti-Bukashkin's dreams are the colour
Of blotting-paper, and couldn't be duller.

Long live Anti-Worlds! They rebut
With dreams the rat-race and the rut.
For some to be clever, some must be boring.
No deserts? No oases, then.

There are no women –
                just anti-men.
In the forests, anti-machines are roaring.
There's the dirt of the earth, as well as the salt.
If the earth broke down, the sun would halt.

Ah, my critics; how I love them.
Upon the neck of the keenest of them,

Fragrant and bald as fresh-baked bread,
There shines a perfect anti-head . . .

. . . I sleep with windows open wide;
Somewhere a falling star invites,
And skyscrapers
                    like stalactites
Hang from the planet's underside.
There, upside down,
                         below me far,
Stuck like a fork into the earth,
Or perching like a carefree moth,
My little Anti-World,
                       there you are!

In the middle of the night, why is it
That Anti-Worlds are moved to visit?

Why do they sit together, gawking
At the television, and never talking?

Neither can understand a word.
How can they bear it? It's too absurd.

Neither can manage the least *bon ton*.
Oh, how they'll blush for it, later on!

Their ears are burning like a pair
Of crimson butterflies, hovering there . . .

. . . A distinguished lecturer lately told me,
'Anti-Worlds are a total loss.'

Still, my apartment-cell won't hold me.
I thrash in my sleep, I turn and toss.

And, radio-like, my cat lies curled
With his green eye tuned in to the world.

DONALD KEENE
(b. 1922)

FROM THE JAPANESE OF KITAHARA HAKASHŪ

Secret Song of the Heretics

I believe in the heretical teachings of a degenerate age, the witchcraft
    of the Christian God,
The captains of the black ships, the marvelous land of the Red Hairs,
The scarlet glass, the sharp-scented carnation,
The calico, arrack, and *vinho tinto* of the Southern Barbarians;
The blue-eyed Dominicans chanting the liturgy who tell me even in
    dreams
Of the God of the forbidden faith, or of the blood-stained Cross,
The cunning device that makes a mustard seed big as an apple,
The strange collapsible spyglass that looks even at Paradise.
They build their houses of stone, the white blood of marble
Overflows in crystal bowls; when night falls, they say, it bursts into
    flame.
That beautiful electrical dream is mixed with the incense of velvet
Reflecting the bird and beasts of the world of the moon.

I have heard their cosmetics are squeezed from the flowers of
    poisonous plants,
And the images of Mary are painted with oil from rotted stones;
The blue letters ranged sideways in Latin or Portuguese
Are filled with a beautiful sad music of heaven.

Oh, vouchsafe unto us, sainted padres of delusion,
Though our hundred years be shortened to an instant, though we die
    on the bloody cross,
It will not matter; we beg for the Secret, that strange dream of
    crimson:
Jesus, we pray this day, bodies and souls caught in the incense of
    longing.

WILLIAM ARROWSMITH
(b. 1924)

FROM THE GREEK OF ARISTOPHANES

I

The Clouds: The Initiation of Strepsiades

So I hereby bequeath you my body,
    for better, dear girls, or worse.
You can shrink me by slow starvation;
    or shrivel me dry with thirst.
You can freeze me or flay me skinless;
    thrash me as hard as you please.
Do any damn thing you've a mind to –
    my only conditions are these:

that when the ordeal is completed,
    a new Strepsiades rise,
renowned to the world as a WELSHER,
    famed as a TELLER OF LIES,

a CHEATER,
        a BASTARD,
                a PHONEY,
                        a BUM,

SHYSTER,
        MOUTHPIECE,
                TINHORN,
                      SCUM,

STOOLIE,
        CON-MAN,
                WINDBAG,
                      PUNK,

OILY,
      GREASY,
             HYPOCRITE,
                  SKUNK,

DUNGHILL,
       SQUEALER,
              SLIPPERY SAM,

FAKER,
     DIDDLER,
            SWINDLER,
                   SHAM,

– or just plain Lickspittle.

And then, dear ladies, for all I care,
    Science can have the body,
to experiment, as it sees fit,
    or serve me up as salami.

Yes, you can serve me up as salami!

2

The Birds: Choral Song

CHORUS   O love,
                   tawnythroat!
           Sweet nightingale,
           musician of the Birds
           Come and sing,
               honey-throated one!
           Come, O love,
               flutist of the Spring,
           accompanying our song.

[*The Chorus turns sharply and faces the audience, while the flute-girl begins the
song of the nightingale at its most mournful. The flute obbligato accompanies the
Chorus throughout.*]

O suffering mankind,
                   lives of twilight,
                               race feeble and fleeting,
like the leaves scattered!
                   Pale generations,
                               creatures of clay,

the wingless, the fading!
Unhappy mortals,
shadows in time,
flickering dreams!
Hear us now,
the ever-living Birds,
the undying,
the ageless ones,
scholars of eternity.
Hear and learn from us
the truth
of all there is to know –
what we are,
and how the gods began,
of Chaos and Dark.
(And when you know
tell Prodikos to go
hang: he's had it!)
There was Chaos at first
and Night and Space
and Tartaros.
There was no Earth.
No Heaven was.
But sable-wingèd Night
laid her wind-egg there
in the boundless lap
of infinite Dark.
And from that egg,
in the seasons' revolving,
Love was born,
the graceful, the golden,
the whirlwind Love
on gleaming wings.
And there in the waste
of Tartaros,
Love with Chaos lay
and hatched the Birds.
We come from Love.
Love brought us to the light.

There were no gods
           till Love had married
                      all the world in love.
Then the world was made.
                Blue Heaven stirred,
                      and Ocean,
the Earth and ageless gods,
                the blessèd ones
                      who do not die.
But we came first.
            We Birds were born
                      the first-born sons of Love,
in proof whereof
            we wear Love's wings,
                      we help his lovers.
How many pretty boys,
                their prime not past,
                      abjuring Love,
have opened up their thighs
                and yielded,
                      overborne by us,
bribed by a Bird,
            a Coot, a Goose,
                  a little Persian Cock!
Think of the services
            we Birds perform
                  for all mankind.
We mark your seasons off,
                summer, spring,
                    winter, fall.
When for Africa
            the screaming Crane departs,
                      you sow your fields.
And then the sailor
            takes his ease
                and hangs his rudder up,
and thief Orestes
            weaves himself a cloak
                  and robs no man.

And then the Kite appears,
                    whose coming says
                              the Spring is here,
the time has come
              to shear the sheep.
                              And so the Swallow
brings his summer,
                when mankind lays
                            its winter weeds away.
And we are Ammon
              and Dodona.
                          We are your Apollo,
that prophetic voice
              to whom you turn
                            in everything you do —
practical affairs,
              commerce and trade,
                          and marriage too.
Birds are your signs,
                and all your omens
                            are governed by Birds:
words are omens
              sent by the Birds.
                          And the same for sneezes,
meetings, asses, voices:
                all are omens,
                          and omens are Birds.
Who are we then
              if we are not
                    your prophetic Apollo?

[*The obbligato of the flute ceases as the Chorus now shifts to a lighter vein and a
quicker tempo.*]

              So elect us as your gods
              and we, in turn, shall be
              your weathervane and Muse,
              your priests of prophecy,
                  foretelling all,
              winter, summer, spring, and fall.

Furthermore, we promise we'll
give mankind an honest deal.
Unlike our smug opponent, Zeus,
we'll stop corruption and abuse.
NO ABSENTEE ADMINISTRATION!
NO PERMANENT VACATION
IN THE CLOUDS!
                    And we promise
to be scrupulously honest.

Last of all, we guarantee
to every single soul on earth,
his sons and their posterity:
          HEALTH
          WEALTH
          HAPPINESS
          YOUTH
          LONG LIFE
          LAUGHTER
          PEACE
          DANCING
            and
          LOTS TO EAT!
We'll mince no words.
Your lives shall be
the milk of the Birds!
We guarantee
you'll all be
revoltingly
          RICH!

O woodland Muse
with lovely throat,
tio tio tio tinx!
who with me sing
whenas in glade or mountain, I,
perched upon the ashtree cry,
tio tio tio tinx!
my tawny-throated song of praise,
to call the Mother to the dance,

a song of joy for blessed Pan,
  tototototototinx!
  whence, like a bee,
the poet stole his honied song,
  my ravished cry,
  tio tio tio tinx!

FROM THE GREEK OF EURIPIDES

The Bacchae Chorus

CHORUS
– When shall I dance once more
 with bare feet the all-night dances,
 tossing my head for joy
 in the damp air, in the dew,
 as a running fawn might frisk
 for the green joy of the wide fields,
 free from fear of the hunt,
 free from the circling beaters
 and the nets of woven mesh
 and the hunters hallooing on
 their yelping packs? And then, hard pressed,
 she sprints with the quickness of wind,
 bounding over the marsh, leaping
 to frisk, leaping for joy,
 gay with the green of the leaves,
 to dance for joy in the forest,
 to dance where the darkness is deepest, where no
  man is.

– What is wisdom? What gift of the gods
 is held in honor like this:
 to hold your hand victorious
 over the heads of those you hate?
 Honor is precious forever.

– Slow but unmistakable
 the might of the gods moves on.
 It punishes that man,

infatuate of soul
and hardened in his pride,
who disregards the gods.
The gods are crafty:
they lie in ambush
a long step of time
to hunt the unholy.
Beyond the old beliefs,
no thought, no act shall go.
Small, small is the cost
to believe in this:
whatever is god is strong:
whatever long time has sanctioned,
that is a law forever;
the law tradition makes
is the law of nature.

— What is wisdom? What gift of the gods
is held in honor like this:
to hold your hand victorious
over the heads of those you hate?
Honor is precious forever.

— Blessèd is he who escapes a storm at sea,
    who comes home to his harbor.
Blessèd is he who emerges from under affliction.
In various ways one man outraces another in the race for wealth
    and power.
Ten thousand men possess ten thousand hopes.
A few bear fruit in happiness; the others go awry.
But he who garners day by day the good of life, he is happiest.
    Blessèd is he.

FROM THE JAPANESE OF HITOMARO

*On going from the province of Iwami, leaving his
wife behind*

Off the cape of Kara
In the weed-locked sea of Iwami,

The sea-pines needle the stones,
The sea-kelp litters the shallows.

And deep as the deep-sea-weed, I long
For my love who leaned sleeping against me,
As the sea-weed leans on the wave:
    (alas, there were not many such nights)
Yet, I have come, left her behind,
Untwined her, like ivy, from me
And now that I bend back with longing,
As the sea-weed bends on the wave,
I cannot see the red sleeves of my love
Through the red-leaved falling confusion
On the oaks of mountain Watari.
Her sleeves have dissolved and gone
As the moon goes under the scud
Of the clouds on mountain Yakami.
The haze is risen. The evening is woven.
        Lo, though I thought myself a man.
The thin stuff of my sleeves is wet with tears.
Envoi:
    My black horse
    Galloping fast
    I have mounted up
    To the scud of the snow-line
    Leaving behind the sleeves of my love.

    O red leaves
    Falling on the autumn hill
    Stop for a while
    Your falling confusion
    Let me see the sleeves of my love.

MICHAEL HAMBURGER
(b. 1924)

FROM THE GERMAN OF GOTTFRIED BENN

I

Night Café

824: The Love and Life of Women.
The 'cello has a quick drink. The flute
belches throughout three beats: his tasty evening snack.
The drum reads on to the end of the thriller.

Green teeth, pimples on his face,
waves to conjunctivitis.

Grease in his hair
talks to open mouth with swollen tonsils,
faith hope and charity round his neck.

Young goiter is sweet on saddle-nose.
He stands her three half pints.

Sycosis buys carnations
to mollify double chin.

B flat minor: sonata op. 35.
A pair of eyes roars out:
Don't splash the blood of Chopin round the place
for this lot to slouch about in!
Hey, Gigi! Stop!

The door dissolves: a woman.
Desert dried out. Canaanite brown.
Chaste. Full of caves. A scent comes with her. Hardly scent.
It's only a sweet leaning forward of the air
against my brain.

A paunched obesity waddles after her.

2

Subway Train

Lascivious shivers. Early bloom. As if
from warm furred skins it wafted from the woods.
A red swarms up. The great strong blood ascends.

Through all of Spring the alien woman walks.
The stocking, stretched, is there. But where it ends
is far from me. I sob upon the threshold:
sultry luxuriance, alien moistures teeming.

O how her mouth squanders the sultry air!
You brain of roses, sea-blood, goddess-twilight,
you bed of earth, how coolly from your hips
your stride flows out, the glide that is in your walking.

Dark: underneath her garments now it lives:
white animal only, loosed, and silent scent.

A wretched braindog, laden down with God.
My forehead wearies me. O that a frame
of clustered blooms would gently take its place,
to swell in unison and stream and shudder.

So lax, adrift. So tired. I long to wander.
The ways all bloodless. Songs that blow from gardens.
Shadows and Flood. Far joys: a languid dying
down into ocean's deep redeeming blue.

FROM THE GERMAN OF GEORG TRAKL

I

Decline

(*To Karl Borromäus Heinrich*)

Over the white pond
The wild birds have travelled on.

In the evening an icy wind blows from our stars.

Over our graves

The broken brow of the night inclines.
Under oak-trees we sway in a silver boat.

Always the town's white walls resound.
Under arches of thorns,
O my brother, blind minute-hands,
We climb towards midnight.

2

Grodek

In the evening the autumn woods cry out
With deadly weapons and the golden plains,
The deep blue lakes, above which more darkly
Rolls the sun; the night embraces
Dying warriors, the wild lament
Of their broken mouths.
But quietly at the meadow's end
Red clouds in which an angry god resides,
The shed blood gathers to itself lunar coolness
All the roads lead to blackest carrion.
Under golden twigs of the night and stars
The sister's shade now sways through the silent copse
To greet the ghosts of the heroes, the bleeding heads;
And softly the dark flutes of autumn sound in the reeds.
O prouder grief! You brazen altars,
Today a great pain feeds the hot flame of the spirit
The grandsons yet unborn.

FROM THE GERMAN OF BERTOLT BRECHT

1

Of Poor B.B.

I, Bertolt Brecht, came out of the black forests.
My mother moved me into the cities while I lay

Inside her body. And the chill of the forests
Will be inside me till my dying day.

In the asphalt city I'm at home. From the very start
Provided with every unction and sacrament:
With newspapers. And tobacco. And brandy.
To the end mistrustful, lazy and content.

I'm polite and friendly to people. I put on
A stiff hat because that's what they do.
I say: they're animals with a quite peculiar smell
And I say: Does it matter? I am too.

Sometimes in the morning on my empty rocking chairs
I'll sit a woman or two, and with an untroubled eye
Look at them steadily and say to them:
Here you have someone on whom you can't rely.

Towards evening it's men that I gather around me
And then we address one another as 'gentlemen'.
They're resting their feet on my table tops
And say: Things will get better for us. And I don't ask: When?

In the gray light before morning the pine-trees piss
And their vermin, the birds, raise their twitter and cheep.
At that hour I drain my glass in town, then throw
The cigar butt away and worriedly go to sleep.

We have sat, an easy generation
In houses thought to be indestructible
(Thus we built those tall boxes on the island of Manhattan
And those thin antennae that amuse the Atlantic swell.)

Of those cities will remain: what passed through them, the wind!
The house makes glad the consumer: he clears it out.
We know that we're only tenants, provisional ones.
And after us there will come: nothing worth talking about.

In the earthquakes to come, I very much hope,
I shall keep my Virginia alight, embittered or no,
I, Bertolt Brecht, carried off to the asphalt cities
From the black forests inside my mother long ago.

2

To Posterity

I

Truly, the age I live in is bleak.
The guileless word is foolish. A smooth brow
Denotes insensitiveness. The laughing man
Has only not yet received
The dreadful news.

What times are these when a conversation
About trees is almost a crime.
Because it includes a silence about so many misdeeds!
That one there calmly crossing the street,
Hasn't he ceased to be at home to
His friends in need?

True enough: I still earn my living.
But, believe me, it's only luck.
Nothing I do gives me the right to eat my fill.
It happens that I've been spared. (When my luck gives out
I shall be lost.)

They tell me: Eat and drink. Be glad that you can!
But how can I eat and drink, when
From the hungry man I snatch what I eat, and
My glass of water deprives the man dying of thirst?
And yet I eat and drink.

And I'd also like to be wise.
In the old books you read what is wise:
To keep out of the strife of the world and spend
Your brief span without fear.
And to refrain from violence
Render good for evil
Not fulfil one's desires, but forget
Is accounted wise.
All these are beyond me:
Truly, the age I live in is bleak.

II

I came into the cities at the time of disorder
When hunger was rife.
I mixed with men at the time of rebellion
And revolted as they did.
So passed the time
Granted to me on earth.

I ate my meals between battles.
I lay down to sleep between the murderers.
Love I pursued unheeding
And on nature looked without patience.
So passed the time
Granted to me on earth.

The streets led into morasses in my time.
Speech betrayed me to the butcher.
There was little I could do. Yet the rulers
Sat more secure but for me, that was my hope.
So passed the time
Granted to me on earth.

My resources were not great. The goal
Lay far ahead.
It was clearly visible, if for me
Scarcely attainable.
So passed the time
Granted to me on earth.

III

You that will emerge from the deluge
In which we drowned,
When you speak of our shortcomings
Remember too
The bleak age
Which you have escaped.

For, changing countries more often than shoes, we walked
Through the wars of the classes, despairing
When there was injustice only and no rebellion.

And yet we know well:
Even hatred of vileness
Distorts a man's features.
Even anger at injustice
Makes hoarse his voice. Ah, we
Who desired to prepare the soil for kindness
Could not ourselves be kind.

But you, when the times permit
Men to be the helpers of men
Remember us
With indulgence.

FROM THE GERMAN OF GÜNTER GRASS

Transformation

Suddenly the cherries were there
although I had forgotten
that cherries exist
and caused to be proclaimed: There never have been cherries –
they were there, suddenly and dear.

Plums fell and hit me,
but whoever thinks
that I was transformed
because something fell and hit me
has never been hit by falling plums.

Only when they poured nuts into my shoes
and I had to walk
because the children wanted the kernels
I cried out for cherries, wanted plums
to hit me – and was transformed a little.

CHRISTOPHER LOGUE
(b. 1926)

FROM THE SPANISH OF PABLO NERUDA

1

'In the hot depth of this summer'

In the hot depth of this summer
The morning is close, storm-filled.

Clouds shift: white rags waving goodbye,
Shaken by the frantic wind as it goes, and

As it goes the wind throbs over us,
Whom love-making has silenced.

Among the trees, like a tongue –
Singing of war or just singing – the wind

Throbs, and the quick sparrow's flight is slapped
By the wind – swift thief, destructive as waves,

Weightless, without form, struck through
And through with flames – which breaks

Soughing its strength out at the gates
Of the enormous silent summer wind.

2

'Drunk as drunk on turpentine'

Drunk as drunk on turpentine
From your open kisses,
Your wet body wedged
Between my wet body and the strake
Of our boat that is made out of flowers,
Feasted, we guide it – our fingers

Like tallows adorned with yellow metal –
Over the sky's hot rim,
The day's last breath in our sails.
Pinned by the sun between solstice
And equinox, drowsy and tangled together
We drifted for months and woke
With the bitter taste of land on our lips,
Eyelids all sticky, and we longed for lime
And the sound of a rope
Lowering a bucket down its well. Then,
We came by night to the Fortunate Isles,
And lay like fish
Under the net of our kisses.

FROM THE GREEK OF HOMER

Sarpedon Falls, Patroclus Exults

(*Iliad*, Book XVI)

Air into azure steel.
The daylight stiffens to translucent horn.
    And through it,
Falling,
    One sun's cord
That opened out into
A radiant cone around Sarpedon's body
And him inside it lying
Like a waxen god asleep on his outstretched hand.
    And his blood broke into hyacinths,
And the sand congealed like moss,
While Glaucus asked:
    'Do you forget your friends so quickly, Hector?
They bleed. You sun your knees. While you are safe,
They die, are stripped, yes, mutilated too,
And the upshot of your caution is
Humiliation to our dead and O, how easily
Ares – the pig-brained butcher god –
Prods his bronze Greek instruments to put
More of us down.
    Sarpedon's dead, my Hector.

Achilles' boy-friend killed him.
And you do nothing? Yet
Not so very long ago you came to him for help,
And all you brought was "*We would be obliged.*"
And "*Thankyou, thankyou,*" when he promised it –
And kept the promise with half Lycia!
And on the day he came, before your dad
Finished his multiplying thanks by previous thanks,
Sarpedon had put on his gear,
Gotten his troops together and engaged the Greeks.
That day and every long successive fighting day
He was first out, last home, with laughter,
Golden wounds, good words, always the first,
First across Agamemnon's ditch today,
And now he's dead and has no fellow
How do you fill your obligations, Hector?'

　　But they had gone.
Rolling across the plain together
Like an arrowhead from a kneeling bowshot . . .
　　Hector, leaning over the horses
As if the chariot was fastened to his belly,
As if his eyes, not horses, drew the Trojans in
Towards the boiling spiral.
　　War.

　　Dust like red mist.
Pain like chalk on slate. Heat like Arctic.
The light withdrawn from Sarpedon's body.
The enemies swirling over it.
Bronze flak.
　　Man against man; banner behind slatted banner;
The torn gold overwhelming the faded blue,
Blue overcoming gold, both up again, both frayed
By arrows that drift like bees, thicker than autumn rain.
　　The left horse falls. The right prances through blades,
Tearing its belly like a silk balloon,
And the shields inch forward under bowshots,
And under the shields the half-lost soldiers think,
'*We fight when the sun rises. When it sets we count the dead.*

What has the beauty of Helen to do with us?' Half-lost,
With the ochre mist swirling around their knees
They shuffle forward, lost, until the shields clash
– AOI!
   Lines of black ovals eight feet high, clash
– AOI!
And in the half-light who will be first to hesitate,
Or, wavering, draw back, and, Yes! . . the slow
Wavering begins and, Yes! . . they bend away from us
As the spears flicker between the black hides,
The bronze glows vaguely, and bones show
Like pink drumsticks.
   And over it all,
As flies shift up and down a Haemorrhage alive with ants,
The captains in their iron masks drift past each other,
Calling, calling, gathering light on their breastplates,
So stained they think that they are colleagues
And do not turn, do not salute, or else salute their enemies.
But we who are under the shields know
Our enemy marches at the head of the column,
And yet we march!
The voice whose orders we obey is the voice of the enemy,
Yet we obey!
And he who is forever talking about enemies
Is himself the enemy!

   Light circling over the dunes. The flying white.
And far above the soldiers the larks soar,
   Treading the cloud, breathing the haze!

   Where is Sarpedon's body? Nobody knows.
   But Glaucus found a man called Bathycles.
He was the richest Greek to sail for Troy.
(Skins and Leathers, a small sword factory, numerous farms)
And thought how very proper it would be
If Glaucus' death became a part of his estate.
   So, to oblige him, Glaucus ran,
And Bathycles (poor fool!) ran after him,
And Glaucus jumped a broken chariot shaft,
And Bathycles jumped – Ahhhhhhhhhhhhhhh! –

And like a woman wets and puts the cotton
Through a needle's eye, Glaucus spun on his pads
And let his javelin through Bathycles.

If Hector waved,
His wounded and his sick got up to fight again;
And if Patroclus called, the Myrmidons
Laughed and called back – with them, as with Patroclus,
To die in battle was like going home.
Inside the yellow spiral
The enemies jammed cheek to cheek,
And both, because they could do nothing else,
Looked up and thought they saw the moon –
Was it so long? – and wondered to themselves,
'*Who will be left to praise us if we win?*
And if we lose, who will there be to bury us?'
Yet it was not the moon they saw through dust,
But the sun
Turning its back upon a day longer than autumn.

> *Try to recall the pause, thock, pause,*
> *Sounds that are made when axeblades follow*
> *Each other through a valuable wood.*
> *Though the work is going on on the far*
> *Side of the valley, and the axeblows are*
> *Muted by a mile of clear, still standing air,*
> *They throb, throb gently in your ears.*
> *And occasionally you can hear a phrase*
> *Spoken between the men who are working*
> *More than a mile away, with perfect clarity.*

Likewise the sounds of
Spear against spear, shield against shield, shield
Against spear around Sarpedon's body.
And nobody, including those who saw him lie
A waxen god asleep on his outstretched hand,
Could know him now,
> *But if you can imagine how*
> *Each evening when the dairy pails are filled*
> *Innumerable flies throng around*
> *The white ruff of the milk*

You will have some idea of how
The Trojans and their enemies
Clouded around Sarpedon's corpse.
   And all this time God watched his favourite enemies;
Minute Patroclus (like a fleck
Of spinning radium on his right hand),
Should he die now? Or push the Trojans back still more?
And on his left, Prince Hector (like a golden mote),
Should he become a coward for an hour
And run for Troy while Patroclus steals Sarpedon's gear?

   The left goes down.
In the half-light Hector's blood turns milky
   And he runs for Troy.

It is true that men are clever.
But the least of gods is cleverer than their best.
   And it was here, before God's hands
(Moons poised either side of the world's agate)
You overreached yourself, Patroclus.
   Yes, my darling,
Not only God was out that day but Lord Apollo.
'*You know he loves the Trojans. So,*
No matter how, how much, how often, or how easily you win,
Once you have forced them back, you stop.'
   Remember it, Patroclus? Or was it years ago
Achilles cautioned you outside his tent?
Remembering or not you stripped Sarpedon's gear,
That glittered like the sea's far edge at dawn,
Ordered your borrowed Myrmidons to drag him off
And went for Troy alone.
   And God turned to Apollo, saying:
'Mousegod, take my Sarpedon out of range
And clarify his wounds with mountain water.
Moisten his body with tinctures of white myrrh
And the sleeping iodine; and when these chrysms dry,
Fold him in minivers that never wear
And lints that never fade,
And call my two blind footmen, Sleep and Death,
And let them carry him to Lycia by Taurus

Where his tribe, playing stone chimes and tambourines,
Will consecrate his royal death,
Before whose memory even the stones shall fade.'
   And Apollo took Sarpedon out of range,
And clarified his wounds with mountain water.
Moistened his body with tinctures of white myrrh
And the sleeping iodine, and when the chrysms dried
The Mousegod folded him in minivers that never wear
And lint that never fades,
And fetched the two blind footmen, Sleep and Death,
And saw they carried him, as fits a man
Before whose memory the stones shall fade,
To Lycia by Taurus.

CHRISTOPHER MIDDLETON
(b. 1926)

FROM THE GERMAN OF MAX HERRMANN-NEISSE

'You Quiet Attender to my Garden'

Where you tread, forget-me-nots come into flower,
you quiet attender to my garden.

You open your hand, and throw the white waves
of seesawing phrases over my mind.

– Thoughts walk armed . . . rank upon rank . . .

In the moon are mills, wintrily orphaned,
as brown as burned, fenced by nerve-light.

– You are asleep? You dream of me? Do fears
trouble your breathing? You feel how I am near?

The night dumbly sings its nameless song.

FROM THE GERMAN OF GEORG TRAKL

To One Who Died Young

O the black angel who softly stepped from the heart of the tree
When we were gentle playmates in the evening,
By the edge of the pale blue fountain.
Our step was easy, the round eyes in autumn's brown coolness,
O the purple sweetness of the stars.

But the other descended the stone steps of the Mönchsberg,
A blue smile on his face, and strangely ensheathed
In his quieter childhood, and died;
And the silver face of his friend stayed behind in the garden,
Listening in the leaves or in the ancient stones.

Soul sang of death, the green decay of the flesh,
And it was the murmur of the forest,
The fervid lament of the animals.
Always from dusky towers rang the blue evening bells.

Times came when the other saw shadows in the purple sun,
The shadows of putrescence in the bare branches;
At nightfall, when by the dusky wall the blackbird sang,
His ghost quietly appeared there in the room.

O the blood that runs from the throat of the musical one,
Blue flower; O the fiery tear
Wept into the night.

Golden cloud and time. In a lonely room
You ask the dead child to visit you more often,
You walk and talk together under elms by the green riverside.

FROM THE GERMAN OF GEORG HEYM

'O boundless, boundless evening'

O boundless, boundless evening. Soon the glow
Of long hills on the skyline will be gone,
Like clear dream country now, rich-hued by sun.
O boundless evening where the cornfields throw
The scattered daylight back in an aureole.
Swallows high up are singing, very small.
On every meadow glitters their swift flight,
In woods of rushes and where tall masts stand
In brilliant bays. Yet in ravines beyond
Between the hills already nests the night.

FROM THE GERMAN OF PAUL CELAN

Fugue of Death

Black milk of daybreak we drink it at nightfall
we drink it at noon in the morning we drink it at night
drink it and drink it
we are digging a grave in the sky it is ample to lie there
A man in the house he plays with the serpents he writes
he writes when the night falls to Germany your golden hair
    Margarete
he writes it and walks from the house the stars glitter he whistles his
    dogs up

he whistles his Jews out and orders a grave to be dug in the earth
he commands us now on with the dance

Black milk of daybreak we drink you at night
we drink in the mornings at noon we drink you at nightfall
drink you and drink you
A man in the house he plays with the serpents he writes
he writes when the night falls to Germany your golden hair
  Margarete
Your ashen hair Shulamith we are digging a grave in the sky it is
  ample to lie there

He shouts stab deeper in earth you there you others you sing and
  you play
he grabs at the iron in his belt and swings it and blue are his eyes
stab deeper your spades you there and you others play on for the
  dancing

Black milk of daybreak we drink you at night
we drink you at noon in the mornings we drink you at nightfall
drink you and drink you
a man in the house your golden hair Margarete
your ashen hair Shulamith he plays with the serpents

He shouts play sweeter death's music death comes as a master from
  Germany
he shouts stroke darker the strings and as smoke you shall climb to
  the sky
then you'll have a grave in the clouds it is ample to lie there

Black milk of daybreak we drink you at night
we drink you at noon death comes as a master from Germany
we drink you at nightfall and morning we drink you and drink you
a master from Germany death comes with eyes that are blue
with a bullet of lead he will hit in the mark he will hit you
a man in the house your golden hair Margarete
he hunts us down with his dogs in the sky he gives us a grave
he plays with the serpents and dreams death comes as a master from
  Germany

your golden hair Margarete
your ashen hair Shulamith

WILLIAM S. MERWIN
(b. 1927)

I

The Gray She-Wolf

As I was in my hut
Painting my shepherd's crook
The Pleiades were climbing
And the moon waning;
Sheep are poor prophets
Not to keep to the fold.
I saw seven wolves
Come up through a dark gully.
They cast lots as they came
To see who should enter the fold;
It fell to an old she-wolf,
Gray, grizzled and bow-legged,
With fangs lifting her lips
Like the points of knives.
Three times she circled the fold
And could take nothing;
Once more she went round it
And snatched the white lamb,
The Merino's daughter,
Niece of the earless ewe,
Which my masters were saving
For Easter Sunday.
– Come here, my seven pups,
Here, my bitch from Trujilla,
Here, you on the chain,
Run down the gray she-wolf.
If you fetch back the lamb
On milk and bread you will dine;
Fail to fetch her back,

You'll dine on my stick. –
On the heels of the she-wolf
They wore their nails down to crumbs;
Seven leagues they ran her
On the harsh mountains.
Climbing a little ravine,
The she-wolf begins to tire:
– Here, dogs, you can take the lamb,
As sound and well as ever. –
– We do not want the lamb
From your wolving mouth;
Your skin is what we want,
For a coat for the shepherd,
Your tail to make laces
To fasten his breeches,
Your head for a bag
To keep spoons in,
And your guts for lute strings
To make the ladies dance.

Fourth Romance *of the Seven Princes of Lara*

(The *romance* is in the person of Gonzalo Gustios,
the Princes' father)

In sorrow I abide in Burgos,
Blind with weeping at my misfortunes,
Not knowing when the day rises
Nor when the night has come,
Were it not that with hard heart
Doña Lambra, who hates me,
Each day as the dawn breaks
Sends to wake my grief also:
So that I may weep for my sons
One by one, every day
She has her men throw
Seven stones at my window.

JAMES MICHIE
(b. 1927)

I

'The history of the long Numantian war'

(*Odes*, Book II, 12)

The history of the long Numantian war;
Iron Hannibal; the sea incarnadined
Off Sicily with Carthaginian gore;
    Wild Lapiths fighting blind-

Drunk Centaurs; or the Giants who made the bright
Halls of old Saturn reel till Hercules
Tamed them – you'd find my gentle lyre too slight
    An instrument for these

Magnificent themes, Maecenas. You can treat
Of Caesar's battles and once bellicose
Chieftains paraded haltered through the street
    Better than I: plain prose

Is called for. My instruction from the Muse is
To sing of your Licymnia's sweet voice,
Her sparkling eyes, and the true heart that chooses
    You and is your dear choice –

A girl who whether she joins the choral dancers,
Or walks with the festal maidens arm-in-arm
On Diana's crowded holy-day, or answers
    A jest, does it with charm.

The wealth of Achaemenes, the Phrygian earth
That made King Midas rich, the Arab lairs
Bursting with treasure – would you rate them worth
    A single one of her hairs

When she bends her neck to your burning mouth? Resist
Soft-stubbornly she may, but even your thirst
To kiss is less than hers is to be kissed,
   And sometimes she drinks first.

2

'*A mob of citizens clamouring for injustice*'

(*Odes*, Book III, 3)

A mob of citizens clamouring for injustice,
An autocrat's grimace of rage, the south wind,
   That moody emperor
Of the wild Adriatic, even the hand

Of Jove who grips the thunder cannot stagger
The just and steady-purposed man. His mind is

   Rock. If the heavens crack
And fall, he'll coolly let the ruin rain.

By this same quality the wandering Hercules
And Pollux stormed the starry ramparts (with them
   Augustus before long
Shall lie and sip the nectar, ruddy-mouthed).

Such courage, Father Bacchus, earned you glory
When, docile-necked, the harnessed tigers drew you
   Westwards. And Romulus,
Who fled from death behind the steeds of Mars,

By that brave action swayed the gods in council
When Juno spoke this welcome: 'Ilium, Ilium,
   A fatal arbiter
Who chose corruptly and a foreign whore

Have turned you into dust: people and paltering
Monarch became my forfeit and the virgin
   Minerva's – doomed the day
Laomedon robbed the gods of payment due.

That worst of guests, the Spartan woman's strutting
Hero, is dead; Hector can bring no help now;
   The house of Priam broke
Its promises, and now the doughty Greeks

Have broken it. The long war, which our quarrels
Made longer still, fades to a whisper. Mars, take
   Your Trojan priestess' child,
My hated grandson. With him I resign

My unrelenting grudge. Let Romulus enter
Our lucent regions, learn the taste of nectar
   And be enrolled with us
In the serene society of gods.

While the broad sea parts Troy and Rome, still raging
Between them, let the refugees be happy
   Ruling what land they please;
As long as cattle trample on the tomb

Of Paris and King Priam and the wild beasts
Hide their whelps safely there, let the great Capitol
   Glitter foursquare and Rome,
The soldier-queen, teach subject Medes the law,

Spreading her name and terror to the limits
Of east and west, from where the mid-sea severs
   Europe from Africa
To where the gross Nile drenches Egypt's soil.

To turn away with scorn from undiscovered
Gold (better left where the earth conceals it) rather
   Than force it to man's use
With snatching, sacrilegious hands – there lies

Her destined source of power. Legions shall push to
The world's fixed ends, eager to see the sights there,
   The frenzied dance of heat
And the cold revelries of mist and storm.

This fortune I foretell for the fierce Romans,
But on these terms: that no fanatic piety

Or overconfidence
Lead them to re-roof their ancestral home.

Should Troy revive, omens of doom shall dog her
And bitter ruin, be renewed. I, sister
    And wife of Jove, myself
Shall head the conquering regiments again.

If Phoebus lets the bronze wall rise a third time,
It shall be levelled by my Greeks a third time,
    And the young captive wife
Shall once more mourn her husband and her sons.'

Where are you rambling, Muse? This theme's beyond your
Light-hearted lyre. End now. Absurd presumption
    To tell tales of the gods
And mar high matters with your reedy voice!

SIMON RAVEN

(b. 1927)

FROM THE LATIN OF HORACE

To Pyrrha

(*Odes*, Book I, 5)

'So who is this wears roses
    And all the scents of May?
And what is the road, my lord, my pretty,
    You take this day?'

'The road I take, old poet,
    Will lead to a bed of down;
For my lady is waiting with tresses of fire
    And a plain silk gown.'

'As yet thy love is a summer's sea,
    And thy ship rides easy of keel,
But when gods turn, then winds are arisen,
    Winds black as steel.

'As yet thy love is calm and kind,
    Thy love is the purest gold:
But a wind is stirring, my lord, my pretty,
    A wind false and cold.

'For I knew her spring and her winter too,
    And scarce escaped from the brine:
I bought hose of worsted and hung my silk
    In Neptune's shrine.'

BURNS SINGER
(b. 1928)
(with Jerzy Peterkiewiez)

FROM THE POLISH OF WACŁAW POTOCKI
Winter, before the War

The frost bit deep. When heavy guns were dragged
Across a marsh no inch of bogland sagged.
The dubious fords raised solid crystal beams.
A glass bridge spanned the deeper parts of streams.
The snow was shameless in its secret keeps
Though clouds had dumped it carelessly in heaps;
But where frost parched it, sparkling silks were spun
And polished lilies to receive the sun.

Someone to whom the war means nothing yet
Glides on a sledge, its runners barely wet,
So light it seems: one horse has leopard spots
And one's hawk-mottled, bird-like as it trots.
A hunter with his hounds treks through the snow.
But, soaking toast in beer by the hearth's glow,
An old man sits. He doesn't want to drive
Off in a sledge. The Spring will soon arrive
And his death with it. Now, since his teeth have gone,
He sucks soaked bread. If any man lives on
Until his youngest grand-daughter gives birth,
This is the last delight he'll find on earth.
In short: the sun reached Capricorn – no more –
And Winter fell from heaven to this hard floor.

FROM THE POLISH OF ZYGMUNT KRASIŃSKI
'*God has denied me the angelic measure*'

God has denied me the angelic measure
That marks a poet in the world of thought.

Had I possessed it earth would become a treasure
But I'm a rhymer since I have it not.

Oh, my heart rings with heavenly zones of sound
But ere they reach my lips they break apart.
Men hear a clattering when I'm around
But day and night I hear my aching heart.

It beats against my waves of blood: a star
Rings in the vast blue whirlpool of the sky.
Men in their festive halls don't hear so far:
God listens to the star until it dies.

FROM THE POLISH OF JOZEF CZECHOWICZ

Grief

My hair is greying but it slants with light
when strands of wind lift it, a chandelier,
that I must always carry through these hollow streets.
The swallows twitter by the river and
it's not so heavy – just my head.
Walk. Walk on.

Walk. Walk. And watch: the scenes, the dreams, the feasts:
cracked glass adorns the synagogues with scars;
a flame gulps up the coarse thick hawser;
the flame of love
denudes us.

The nations are most greedy when they roar.
They cannot whimper like a hungry man.

This evening heavily upon the world
spreads its low length as nostrils scent
red milk from bared volcanoes.
Deciphering which stranger: Who are you?
and multiplying magically through
our own torn selves, I shoot my names, and die.
I die, who huddled with my plough in furrows;

I, a brisk lawyer, drown in instructions;
I, in chlorine, I choking, I dying, gas!
and I am the girl who sleeps with the primrose;
and I, a child, in a live torch, live;
and I at my market stall with the blaze of a bomb;
and I am the madman who's hanged for the fire:
I am my signature, my mother's illiterate cross.

But now the harvest
glows with deep noise.

And how can the river untorture itself and unrust
our brotherly blood before, among us,
the colonnades rise, the mathematical eagles?
A blizzard of swallows will come
with a whirl that swirls my head,
but through the darkness that the birds give wing
I shall walk, I shall walk on.

EDMUND KEELEY
(b. 1928)

AND

PHILIP SHERRARD
(b. 1922)

FROM THE
MODERN GREEK OF ANGHELOS SIKELIANOS

The First Rain

We leaned from the open window.
All was one with our mood.
Sulphur-pale, the clouds
made field and vineyard dark,
with secret turbulence
wind moaned in the trees,
and the quick swallow went
breasting across the grass.
Then suddenly the thunder
broke, and tore the sky,
and dancing came the rain.
The dust leapt in the air.
We, as our nostrils felt
the teeming earth-smell, held
our lips open, to let it
water deep in the breast.
Then, side by side, our faces
as mullen and as the olive
already wet with rain:
'What smell,' we asked, 'is this,
that bee-like rends the air?
From balsam, pine, acanthus,
osier or the thyme?'
So was it, that, as I breathed,

sweetness filled my mouth,
I stood, a lyre, caressed
by its profusion, till,
meeting again your gaze,
blood clamoured in every vein.
I bent above the vine,
leaf-shuddering, to drink
its honey and its flower:
nor could I – my mind a dense
grape-cluster, bramble-caught the breath –
single those smells, but reaped
and gathered all, and all
drank as one does from fate
sorrow or sudden joy;
I drank them down, and when
I touched your waist, my blood
like the nightingale sang out
and ran like all the waters.

FROM THE MODERN GREEK OF ODYSSEUS ELYTIS

I

The Mad Pomegranate Tree

Inquisitive matinal high spirits
à perdre haleine

In these all-white courtyards where the south wind blows
Whistling through vaulted arcades, tell me, is it the mad pomegran-
ate tree
That leaps in the light, scattering its fruitful laughter
With windy wilfulness and whispering, tell me, is it the mad pome-
granate tree
That quivers with foliage newly born at dawn
Raising high its colours in a shiver of triumph?
On plains where the naked girls awake,
When they harvest clover with their light brown arms

Roaming round the borders of their dreams – tell me, is it the mad
    pomegranate tree,
Unsuspecting, that puts the lights in their verdant baskets
That floods their names with the singing of birds – tell me
Is it the mad pomegranate tree that combats the cloudy skies of the
    world?

On the day that it adorns itself in jealousy with seven kinds of
    feathers,
Girding the eternal sun with a thousand blinding prisms
Tell me, is it the mad pomegranate tree
That seizes on the run a horse's mane of a hundred lashes,
Never sad and never grumbling – tell me, is it the mad pomegranate
    tree
That cries out the new hope now dawning?

Tell me, is that the mad pomegranate tree waving in the distance,
Fluttering a handkerchief of leaves of cool flame,
A sea near birth with a thousand ships and more,
With waves that a thousand times and more set out and go
To unscented shores – tell me, is it the mad pomegranate tree
That creaks the rigging aloft in the lucid air?

High as can be, with the blue bunch of grapes that flares and cele-
    brates
Arrogant, full of danger – tell me, is it the mad pomegranate tree
That shatters with light the demon's tempests in the middle of the
    world
That spreads far as can be the saffron ruffle of day
Richly embroidered with scattered songs – tell me, is it the mad
    pomegranate tree
That unfastens with haste the silk apparel of day?

In petticoats of April first and cicadas of the feast of mid-August
Tell me, that which plays, that which rages, that which can entice
Shaking out of threats their evil black darkness
Spilling in the sun's embrace intoxicating birds
Tell me, that which opens its wings on the breast of things
On the breast of our deepest dreams, is that the mad pomegranate
    tree?

2

The Body of Summer

A long time has passed since the last rain was heard
Above the ants and lizards
Now the sun burns endlessly
The fruit paints its mouth
The pores in the earth open slowly
And beside the water that drips in syllables
A huge plant gazes into the eye of the sun.

Who is he that lies on the shores beyond
Stretched on his back, smoking silver-burnt olive leaves?
Cicadas grow warm in his ears
Ants are at work on his chest
Lizards slide in the grass of his arm pits
And over the seaweed of his feet a wave rolls lightly
Sent by the little siren that sang:

'O body of summer, naked, burnt
Eaten away by oil and salt
Body of rock and shudder of the heart
Great ruffling wind in the osier hair
Breath of basil above the curly pubic mound
Full of stars and pine needles
Body, deep vessel of the day!

'Soft rains come, violent hail
The land passes lashed into the claws of the north wind
Which darkens in the depths with furious waves
The hills plunge into the dense udders of the clouds
And yet behind all this you laugh carefree
And find your deathless moment again
As the sun finds you again on the sandy shores
As the sky finds you again in your naked health.'

FROM THE MODERN GREEK OF NIKOS GATSOS

I

'They say the mountains tremble . . .'

They say the mountains tremble and the fir-trees rage
When night gnaws the tile-pins to let in the kallikantzari
When hell gulps down the torrents' foaming toil
Or when the groomed hair of the pepper-tree becomes the North-
    Wind's plaything.

Only Achaian cattle graze vigorous and strong
On abundant fields in Thessaly beneath an ageless, watching sun
They eat green grass and celery, leaves of the poplar tree, they drink
    clear water in the troughs
They smell the sweat of the earth and then fall heavily to sleep in the
    shade of the willow tree.

Cast out the dead said Heraclitus yet he too saw the sky turn pale
Saw two small cyclamens kissing in the mud
And as the wolf comes down from the forests to see the dog's carcass
    and weep,
He too fell to kiss his own dead body on the hospitable soil.
What good to me the bead that glistens on your forehead?
I know the lightning wrote its name upon your lips
I know an eagle built its nest within your eyes
But here on this damp bank there is one way only
One deceptive way yet you must take it

You must plunge into blood before time forestalls you,
Cross over opposite to find your companions again
Flowers birds deer
To find another sea, another tenderness,
To take Achilles' horses by the reins
Instead of sitting dumb scolding the river
Stoning the river like the mother of Kitso
Because you too will be lost and your beauty will have aged.
I see your childhood shirt drying on the branches of a willow
Take it, this flag of life, to shroud your death
And may your heart not fail you

And may your tear not fall upon this pitiless earth
As a penguin's tear once fell in the frozen wilderness
Complaint achieves nothing
Life will always be the same
With the serpent's flute in the land of phantoms
With the song of brigands in aromatic groves
With the knife of some sorrow in the cheek of hope
With the pain of some spring in a wood-owl's heart.
As long as a sharp sickle and plough are found in a joyful hand
As long as a little wheat flowers for the feasts
A little wine for remembrance, a little water for the dust.

2

'In the griever's courtyard . . .'

In the griever's courtyard no sun rises
Only worms appear to mock the stars
Only horses sprout upon the ant hills
And bats eat birds and cast off sperm.

In the griever's courtyard night never sets
Only the foliage vomits forth a river of tears
When the devil passes by to mount the dogs
And the crows swim in a well of blood.

In the griever's courtyard the eye has gone dry
The brain has frozen and the heart turned to stone
Frog-flesh hangs from the spider's teeth
Hungry locusts scream at the vampire's feet.

In the griever's courtyard black grass grows
Only one night in May did a breeze pass through
A step light as a tremor on the meadow
A kiss of the foam-trimmed sea.

And should you thirst for water, we will wring a cloud
And should you hunger for bread, we will slaughter a nightingale
Only wait a moment for the wild rue to open,
For the black sky to flash, the mullen to flower.

But it was a breeze that vanished, a lark that disappeared
It was the face of May, the moon's whiteness
A step light as a tremor on the meadow
A kiss of the foam-trimmed sea.

NATHANIEL TARN
(b. 1928)

FROM THE SPANISH OF PABLO NERUDA

Leviathan

Ark, wrathful peace, night of the brute
awash, alien antarctica,
you will not pass me by
heaving your berg of shadows without one day
my entering your walls and dredging up
your armature of sunken winters.

Your sombre fire spat south,
blown, exiled planet, your silent territories
shifting sargassos and shaking up
the solid ages of the sea.

Form throbbed alone, a hugeness sealed
by tremors in the world through which would glide
your hide of majesty, frightened itself
by its own potency and tenderness.

Shrine harsh with rage
fired by the torches of the charcoal snows,
when your blind blood was molten
the sea's antiquity slept in its gardens,
the moon in its reflection flew, unravelling
her tail of phosphorescent loadstones.
Life crackled
in blue bonfires, mother-medusa,
multiplied tempest of ovaries,
and all that flowering was purity,
a palpitation in the ocean's tendrils.

So was your forest of masts
arrayed among the waters
like the passing of maternity over blood

314

and your power was immaculate night,
a sea-slide flooding of roots.
Terror and maps made mad shivered your solitude:
your continent sheered off
beyond the hoped-for islands;
yet terror glazed the breasts
of the iced moon, biting into your flesh,
invested solitudes which gave asylum
to your tremendous beacon now blown out.
Night was with you and clung to you
like tempestuous silt,
your whirlwind-withered tail
churning the ice in which the stars were sleeping.

Oh great and gashed! fountain of fire
whirling its ruined thunders
within the tethering of the harpoon,
dyed in your blood bath, drained of your life
drowsy and gentle beast
lugged like a maelstrom of ruptured hemispheres
to the black blubber ships
peopled by rancour and plague.

> Oh great statue, dead among crystals
> of the polar moon, filling the sky
> with a lamenting, terrorizing cloud
> that blankets the ocean with blood.

PETER H. LEE
(b. 1929)

FROM THE KOREAN OF YI YUKSA

The Summit

Beaten by the bitter season's whip,
At last I am driven to this north.

I stand upon the sword-blade frost,
Where numb sky and plateau merge.

I do not know where to bend my knees,
Nor where to lay my vexed steps.

I cannot but close my eyes and think –
Winter, O winter is a steel rainbow.

FROM THE KOREAN OF KIM KWANG-GYUN

The Sunflower

Here is the white sunflower –
Its tyranny caused a small village to fade;
In the old house by the village road,
A hoary mother turned a water wheel.

When twilight tumbled down the purple lane,
The rushes by the stream
Shook their heads and wept.

To light the lamp on our father's tomb,
Nightly I led my blind sister by the hand
And crossed the track dyed by the moonlight.

FROM THE KOREAN OF SŎ CHŎNG-JU

Self-Portrait

Father was a serf, seldom came home at night.
At home my grandmother, old as
The shriveled root of leek,
And a blossoming date tree.
Big with child, Mother wanted just one apricot.

I was a mother's son with dirty fingernails
Under a lamp by the mud wall.
With bushy hair and staring eyes,
I am said to resemble Grandpa on Mother's side,
Who in 1894 went to sea and never returned.

For twenty-three years the wind has reared two-thirds of me,
And the world has become a more embarrassing place.
Some have read a convict in my eyes,
Others an idiot in my mouth.
Yet I will repent nothing.

At each dawn, brightly assailing,
The dews of poetry settled on my brow,
Mixed with drops of blood.
And I have come this far panting
Like a sick dog with his tongue hanging out
In the sun and in the shade.

KENNETH McROBBIE

(b. 1929)

(with Ilona Duczyńska)

FROM THE HUNGARIAN OF FERENC JUHÁSZ

The Boy Changed into a Stag Cries out at the Gate of Secrets

Her own son the mother called
from afar crying,
her own son the mother called
from afar crying,
she went before the house, from there calling
her hair's full knot she loosed,
with it the dusk wove a dense quivering
veil, a precious cloak down to her ankles,
wove a stiff mantle, heavy-flaring,
a flag for the wind with ten black tassels
a shroud, the fire-stabbed, blood-tainted dusk.
Her fingers she twined in the sharp tendrilled
stars, her face the moon's foam coated
and on her own son she called shrilly
as once she called him, a small child,
she went before the house and talked to the wind,
with song birds spoke, sending swiftly
words after the wild pairing geese
to the shivering bullrushes,
to the potato-flower so silvery,
to the clench-balled bulls, rooted so firmly,
to the well-shading fragrant sumach tree,
she spoke to the fish leaping at play,
to the mauve oil-rings afloat fleetingly:
          You birds and boughs, hear me
listen as I cry out,
          and listen, you fishes, you flowers
listen for I speak to be heard,
          listen you glands of expanding soils

you vibrant fins, astral-seeding parachutes,
decelerate, you humming motors of the saps
in the depth of the atom, screw down the whining taps.
All metal-pelvised virgins, sheep alive under cotton
listen as I cry out,
for I'm crying out to my son!

Her own son the mother called
her cry ascending in a spiral,
within the gyre of the universe it rose
Her limbs flashing in the light rays
like the back of a fish all slippery scaled,
or a roadside boil of salt or crystal.
Her own son the mother called:
Come back, my own son, come back
　　I call you, your own mother!
Come back, my own son, come back
　　I call you, your mild harbour,
come back, my own son, come back
　　I call you, your cool fountain,
come back, my own son, come back
　　I call you, your memory's teat,
come back, my own son, come back
　　I call you, your withered tent,
come back, my own son, come back
　　I call you, your almost sightless lamp.

Come back, my own son, for I'm blind in this world of sharp
　　objects
within yellow-green bruises my eyes are sinking, my brow contracts,
my thighs – my barked shins
from all sides things rush at me like crazed wethers,
the gate, the post, the chair try their horns on me
doors slam upon me like drunken brawlers,
the perverse electricity shoots its current at me
my flaking skin seeps blood – a bird's beak cracked with a stone,
　　scissors swim out of reach like spider crabs, all metal
the matches are sparrows' feet, the pail swings back at me with its
　　handle,
come back, my own son, come back

my legs no longer carry me like the young hind,
    vivid tumours pout on my feet
    gnarled tubers penetrate my purpling thighs,
on my toes grow bony structures,
    the fingers on my hands stiffen, already the shelly flesh
scales off like slate from aging geologic formations,
    every limb has served its time and sickens
come back, my own son, come back,
    for I am no more as I was,
    I am gaunt with inner visions
    which flare from the stiffening hoary organs
    as on winter mornings an old cock's crowing
ings from a fence of shirts, hanging hard-frozen,
 call you, your own mother,
ome back, my own son, come back,
to the unmanageable things bring a new order,
discipline the estranged objects, tame the knife,
    domesticate the comb,
for I am now but two gritty green eyes
glassy and weightless like the *libellula*
whose winged nape and dragon jaws, you know it well
    my son, hold so delicately
two crystal apples in his green-lit skull,
I am two staring eyes without a face
seeing all, now one with unearthly beings.
Come back, my own son, come back,
    with your fresh breath, set all to rights again.

        In the far forest, the lad heard
        at once, he jerked up his head
        with his wide nostrils testing
        the air, soft dewlaps pulsing
        with veined ears pricked, harkening
        alertly to those tones sobbing
        as to a hunter's slimy tread,
        or hot wisps curling from the bed
        of young forest fires, when smoky
        high woods start to whimper bluely.
        He turned his head, no need to tell

him, this was the voice he knew so well,
now by an agony he's seized
fleece on his buttocks he perceives,
in his lean legs sees the proof
of strange marks left by each cleft hoof,
where lilies shine in forest pools
see his low, hairy-pursed buck-balls.
He pushes his way down to the lake
breasting the brittle willow brake
rump slicked with foam, at each bound
he slops white froth on the hot ground,
his four black hooves tear out a path
through wild flowers wounded to death,
stamp a lizard into the mould
neck swollen, tail snapped, growing cold
and when he reached the lake at last
into its moonlit surface glanced:
it holds the moon, beeches shaking
and back at him a stag staring.
Only now thick hair does he see
covering all his slender body
hair over knees, thighs, the transverse
tasselled lips of his male purse,
his long skull had sprouted antlers
into bone leaves their bone boughs burst,
his face is furry to the chin
his nostrils are slit and slant in.
Against trees his great antlers knock
veins knot in ropes along his neck,
madly he strains, prancing he tries
vainly to raise an answering cry,
only a stag's voice bells within
the new throat of this mother's son,
he drops a son's tears, paws the brink
to banish that lake-monster, sink
it down into the vortex sucking
fluid dark, where scintillating
little fish flash their flowery fins,
minute, bubble-eyed diamonds.

The ripples subside at last in the gloom,
but a stag still stands in the foam of that
     moon.
Now in his turn the lad cried back
     stretching up his belling neck,
now in his turn the lad called back
     through a stag's throat, through the fog calling:
     Mother, my mother
     I cannot go back,
     mother, my mother
     you must not lure me,
     mother, my mother
     my dear breeding nurse,
     mother, my mother
     sweet frothy fountain,
     safe arms that held me
     whose heavy breasts fed me
     my tent, shelter from frosts,
     mother, my mother
     seek not my coming,
     mother, my mother
     my frail silken stalk,
     mother, my mother
     bird with teeth of gold,
     mother, my mother,
     you must not lure me!
     If I should come home
     my horns would drag you
     from horn to sharp horn
     I'd toss your body,
     if I should come home
     down I would roll you,
     tread your loose veiny
     breasts, mangled by hooves,
     I'd stab with unsheathed
     horns, maul with my teeth
     tread in your womb, even.
     If I should come home
     mother, my mother

I'd spill out your lungs
for blue flies buzzing round,
and the stars would stare down
into your flower-organs,
which once did hold me,
with warmth of summer suns
in shiny peace encased
where warmth never ceased,
as once cattle breathed
gently to warm Jesus.
Mother, my mother
do not summon me,
death would strike you down
in my shape's coming
if this son drew near.
Each branch of my antlers
is a gold filament,
each prong of my antlers
a winged candlestick,
each tine of my antlers
a catafalque candle,
each leaf of my antlers
a gold-laced altar.
Dead surely you'd fall
if you saw my grey antlers
soar into the sky
like the All Soul's Eve
candle-lit graveyard,
my head a stone tree
leafed with growing flame.
Mother, my mother
if I came near you
I would soon singe you
like straw, I would scorch
you to greasy black clay,
you'd flare like a torch
for I would roast you
to charred shreds of flesh.
Mother, my mother

do not summon me
for if I came home
I would devour you,
for if I came home
your bed I would ravage,
the flower garden
with my thousand-pronged
horns would I savage,
I'd chew through the trees
in the stag-torn groves,
drink dry the one well
in a single gulp,
if I should return
I'd fire your cottage,
and then I would run
to the old graveyard,
with my pointed soft
nose, with all four hooves
I'd root up my father,
with my teeth wrench off
his cracked coffin lid
and snuff his bones over!
Mother, my mother
do not lure me,
I cannot go back,
for if I came home
I'd bring your death surely.

In a stag's voice the lad cried
and in these words his mother answered him:
    Come back, my own son, come back
I call you, your mother.
    Come back my own son, come back
I'll cook you brown broth, and you'll slice onion-rings in it
they'll crunch between your teeth, like quartz splintering in a giant's
                                         jaws,
I'll give you warm milk in a clean jug,
from my last keg trickle wine into heron-necked bottles
and I know how to knead the bread with my rocky fists, I know how
                                        you like it

bread for baking soft-bellied buns for you, sweet bread for the feasts.
    Come back, my own son, come back,
from the live breasts of screeching geese for your eiderdown
                    I plucked feathers,
weeping I plucked my weeping geese, the spots stripped of
                    feathers turning
a fierce white on their breasts, like the mouths of the dying,
I shook up your pallet in the clear sunlight, made it fresh
                for your rest,
the yard has been swept, the table is laid – for your coming.

Mother, my mother
    for me there's no homecoming,
do not lay out for me twisted white bread
    or sweet goat's milk in my flowered mug foaming,
and do not prepare for me a soft bed,
    for their feathers ravage not the breasts of the geese,
spill your wine rather, upon my father's grave let it soak in,
    the sweet onions bind into a garland,
fry up for the litfle ones that froth-bellying dough.
      The warm milk would turn to vinegar at my
              tongue's lapping
      into a stone turtle you'd see the white bread changing
      your wine within my tumbler like red blood rising,
      the eiderdown would dissolve into little blue flames
          in silence
      and the brittle-beaked mug splinter into swordgrass.
O mother, O mother, my own good mother
    my step may not sound in the paternal house,
I must live deep in the green wood's underbrush
    no room for my tangled antlers in your shadowy
house, no room in your yard for my cemetery
    antlers, for my foliated horns are a loud world-tree
their leaves displaced by stars, their green moss by the
              Milky Way.
    Sweet-scented herbs must I take in my mouth, only
the first-growth grasses can my spittle liquefy,
    I may no longer drink from the flowered mug you bring
only from a clean spring, only from a clean spring!

I do not understand, do not understand your strange tortured
                                    words, my son
you speak like a stag, a stag's soul seems to possess you, my
                                    unfortunate one.
When the turtle-dove cries, the turtle-dove cries, when the little
                                    bird sings, the little bird sings,
                                    my son
wherefore am I – in the whole universe am I the last lost
                                    soul left, the only one?
Do you remember, do you remember your small once-young
                                    mother, my son?
I do not grasp, do not grasp your sad tortured words my long
                                    lost son.

Do you remember how you came running, running home to me
                                    so happy with your school report,
        you dissected a bull-frog, spreading out on the fence his
                                    freckled webbed paddle-feet,
and how you pored over the books on aircraft, how you followed
                                    me in to help with the washing,
        you were in love with Irene B., your best friend was V. J.,
        and there was H. S., the wild orchid-bearded painter,
and do you remember on Saturday nights, when your father came
                                    home sober, how happy you were?

O mother, my mother, do not speak of my sweetheart of old
                                    or of my friend
        like fish they fleet by in cold depths,
                                    the vermilion-chinned painter
        who knows now where he has gone his shouting way, who
                                    knows mother, where my youth
                                    has gone?
Mother, my mother, do not recall my father, out of his flesh
                                    sorrow has sprouted,
        sorrow blossoms from the dark earth, do not recall
                                    my father, my father,
        from the grave he'd rise, gathering about him his
                                    yellowed bones,
        from the grave stagger, hair and nails growing anew.

Oh! Oh! Uncle Wilhelm came, the coffin-maker, that
                                  puppet-faced man,
    he told us to take your feet and drop you neatly in the coffin.
    I retched because I was afraid. I had come straight home
                                  from Pest that day.
    You too, my father, went back and forth to Pest, you were
                                  only an office messenger. The
                                  rails twisted up.
    Oh, the stabbing knives in my belly then, shadows from the
                                  candle ravined your tight cheeks,
your new son-in-law, Laci the barber, shaved you that day, the
                                  candle dribbling the while like
                                  a silent baby
    regurgitating its glistening entrails, its long luminous nerves
                                  like vines.
    The choral society stood round you in their purple hats,
                                  mourning you at the tops of
                                  their voices,
    with one finger I traced the rim of your forehead.
                                  Your hair was alive still,
    I heard it grow, I saw the bristles sprout from your chin
    blackened by morning, the next day your throat had sunk
                                  beneath snake-grass stalks of hair
    its curve like a soft-furred cantaloup, the colour of a yellow
                                  haired caterpillar upon blue
                                  cabbage skin.
Oh, and I thought your hair, your beard, would overgrow
                                  the whole room, the yard
    the entire world, stars nestling like cells in its hiving strands.
Ah! Heavy green rain started then to fall, the team of red
                                  horses before the hearse neighed
                                  in terror,
    one lashing out above your head with a lightning bolt hoof,
                                  the other relentlessly pissing
    so that his purple parts passed out with it like a hanged
                                  man's tongue, while their
                                  coachman cursed

and the downpour washed round the huddled brassbandsmen.
Then all those old friends blew
with a will
sobbing as they played, beside the globe-thistle studded
chapel wall,
those old friends blew till their lips swelled blue, and the tune
spiralled out and up,
the old friends blew with those cracked lips bleeding now,
with eyeballs staring,
blew for the card games and booze, the bloated, the withered
and the trumped women,
played you out for the red-letter day beer-money, the tips
sent whirling into space after you
they blew, sobbing as they blew sadly down into the
sedimentary layers of silted
sadness,
music pouring from the burnished mouths, from rings of brass
into putrescent nothingness,
out of it streamed the petrified sweethearts, rotting women,
and mouldy grandfathers in
the melody,
with small cottages, cradles, and rolling like onions a
generation of enamel-swollen,
silver-bodied watches,
Easter bells and multifarious saviours there came also on
wide-spreading wings of sound
that summoned up satchels, railway wheels, and soldiers
brass-buttoned at the salute,
the old friends played on, teeth reddening under lips curled
back and swollen like
blackened liver,
and yourself conducting the choir – Well done, boys, that's
grand, carry it on, don't stop now!
all the time, with hands clasped tight, those gold spiders with
huge legs knotted like spoke-
joints, resting on your heart,
in the cupboard your collapsed boots await the relations,
white socks naked on your
bread-crust curling feet,

old friends that day played you out in the crashing rain,
                         valves snapping like steel Adam's
                         apples
    like fangs of antediluvian birds, teeth of the *Carcharodon*
                         looking for carrion from those
                         brass trumpets,
O mother, my mother, do not recall my father
    let my father be, lest his eyes burst out of the
                         reopening earth.

    Her own son the mother called
        from afar crying:
    Come back, my own son, come back
        turn away from that stone-world
    you stag of the stone-woods, the industrialized air,
                         electric grids,
        chemical lightenings, iron bridges, and streetcars lap up
                         your blood,
            day by day they make a hundred assaults on you,
                         yet you never hit back,
        it is I calling you, your own mother
            come back, my own son, come back.

    There he stood on the renewing crags of time,
    stood on the ringed summit of the sublime
    universe, there stood the lad at the gate of secrets,
    his antler prongs were playing with the stars,
    with a stag's voice down the world's lost paths
    he called back to his life-giving mother:
        Mother, my mother, I cannot go back
    pure gold seethes in my hundred wounds,
    day by day, a hundred bullets knock me from my feet
    and day by day I rise again, a hundred times more complete,
    day by day I die three billion times,
    day by day I'm born three billion times,
    each prong of my antlers is a dual-based pylon,
    each branch of my antlers a high-tension wire,
    my eyes are ports for ocean-going merchantmen, my veins
                         are tarry cables, these
    teeth are iron bridges, and in my heart the surge of
                         monster-infested seas,

each vertebra is a teeming metropolis, for a spleen I have a
                  smoke-puffing barge
each of my cells is a factory, my atoms are solar systems
sun and moon swing in my testicles, the Milky Way is
                  my bone marrow,
each point of space is one part of my blood
my brain's impulse is out in the curling galaxies.

Lost son of mine, come back for all that – Oh, come back,
sleepless your mother's eyes shall watch on for you still.

Only to die will I return, only to die come back,
yes, I will come, will come to die
and when I have come – but to die – my mother
then may you lay me in the parental house,
with your marbled hand you may wash my body
and my glandulous eyelids close with a kiss.
      And then, when my flesh falls apart
and lies in its own stench, yet deep in flowers
      then shall I feed on your blood, be your body's fruit
then shall I be your own small son again,
and this shall give pain to you alone mother,
      to you alone, O my mother.

GEORGE MacBETH
(b. 1932)

FROM THE FRENCH OF FRANCIS PONGE

The Wasp Woman

XIV

First there was the furnace. And then
the half-charred wasp was born, hissing, terrible
    and by no means a matter
of indifference to Men-kind, for they faced

in her burning elegance their abortive
    hunger for speed and for closed
flight through air. And in mine I saw an earthed fire

whose wings gushed out in all directions, and on
    unforeseen trajectories.
It burned as if on offensive missions from

a nest in the ground. Like an engine out of
    control, sometimes it trembled
as though she were not the mistress of her own

destructiveness. So at first that fire spread in
    the earth, crackling, fluttering:
and then when the wings were accomplished, the sexed

wings, the antennaed squadrons broke out on their
    deadly business into the
flesh, and their work began to be finished, I

mean, her crime.

XV

In her swarm of words, the abrupt
    waspishness. But wait. Was this
devised flutter in the trench any more than

the weak rebellion of a few seeds, outraged
   by their sower? It was their —
own violence that first brought them into his

apron. No, go back. This was a fire whose wings
   gushed out in all directions,
and on unforeseen trajectories. And I

faced in her burned elegance my abortive
   hunger for speed and for closed
flight through air. Or must one look further. Here was

the natural world on the wing. Her cruel
   divisions preparing their
offensive against male tyranny. I bared

my forests for their sting. But already her
   banked animosity was
flowing away in random fury. . . .

INDEX TO AUTHORS

and titles of Anonymous Works

BY PHILIP WARD